The Happiness Factor

The Happiness Factor

...and how to get it

John Partington

with

Shane Dean

New Wine Press

New Wine Ministries
PO Box 17
Chichester
West Sussex
United Kingdom
PO19 2AW

Scripture quotations are taken from the following versions of the Bible:

NIV – The Holy Bible, New International Version. Copyright © 1973, 1978,
1984 by International Bible Society. Used by permission of Hodder and
Stoughton Limited.

NKJV – The Holy Bible, New King James Version. Copyright © 1982 by
Thomas Nelson Inc.

NLT – Holy Bible, New Living Translation. Copyright © 1996, 2004 by
Tyndale Charitable Trust. Used by permission of Tyndale House Publishers.

RSV – Revised Standard Version. Copyright © 1946, 1952 by the Division of
Christian Education of the National Council of the Churches of Christ in the
United States of America.

KJV – King James Version. Crown copyright.

ISBN 13: 978–1–903725–80–1
ISBN 10: 1–903725–80–1

Typeset by CRB Associates, Reepham, Norfolk
Cover design by CCD, www.ccdgroup.co.uk
Printed in Malta

Contents

Acknowledgements

To my wife Andrene, my three great children, Aaron, Heidi and Bethany – a big thank you for accepting me for who I am and being my very best friends!

A big thank you too, to Shane Dean, my former PA and good pal, whose insistence and hard work has resulted in this book being written.

Foreword

When writing any book, the author draws upon their knowledge and experience of the subject covered. I have been blessed/fortunate to live a fantastic life, in which even the problems and difficulties have been overshadowed by joy through adopting many of the principles and truths uncovered in these pages.

The Happiness Factor was written out of a desire for people to enjoy their lives. Sadly, most people don't seem to. We've become a "pill-popping", therapy-seeking, unhappy generation where discontentment and depression are too common and suicide rates are rocketing. People are dying without ever finding real life.

It doesn't have to be that way.

The Happiness Factor will show you the A to Z of how to get overflowing happiness in your life. It will show ways in which you can live life to the full. More than that it will help you to spread happiness throughout your family and friends. Happiness is within your grasp and the prescription is simple – but it can take time to develop the habits that will help you keep it. *The Happiness Factor* will give you a practical, step-by-step method of taking hold of it and keeping it for good.

Remember, life is short, so let's live each day as if it were potentially our last and let's fill it with meaning, purpose and laughter!

Be Happy,

John

CHAPTER 1

Finding the H Factor

If you're not crazy then you undoubtedly want to be happy, and you're not alone. Happiness is what everyone in the world wants and it has prompted philosophers for thousands of years to dedicate their lives to discover a "happiness prescription". Sadly, the majority have failed. Scientific investigations have proven that people who are happy earn more, feel younger, live on average seven years longer, feel healthier, have fewer colds, lower blood pressure and lower levels of the damaging stress hormone, cortisol. They also enjoy life so much more than those who are unhappy.

> **Those with the H Factor have *happiness*. Not just standard, run-of-the-mill, normal happiness, but something much, much more. And everyone can have it.**

A Prescription for Happiness

I believe I've got the secret of happiness which I've called "The H Factor". We hear so much about the X Factor – that rare something that certain people are born with – but the H Factor is different altogether.

Those with the H Factor have *happiness*. Not just standard, run-of-the-mill, normal happiness, but something much, much more. And everyone can have it. That is why I wrote this book. It's an A to Z guide in twenty-six short chapters to help you feel life-to-the-full happiness and to see it overflow in your world, among your family, friends, colleagues and wherever you go.

I believe I've got the H Factor and I passionately want others to have the same thing. The principles used to get it – listed in the twenty-six chapters – have been tried and tested since my early teens. Although I am a Christian, these nuggets of happiness wisdom are for you whether you're an atheist, agnostic or antique collector! There is nothing quite like having the H Factor.

How Does it Feel?

Imagine looking forward to every day and enjoying every minute of your life. Happiness is not just for princesses in fairy stories, the wealthy, the muscle-bound or the beautiful. I can say this with certainty as I'm not in any of those categories!

So what does the H Factor feel like? Well, it's a feeling like no other. You feel you can conquer the world. Nothing can stop you. Other people flock around you and want what you have. You eagerly await the start of each day. You hear the birds singing and appreciate the beauty around you. Your relationships thrive. Your marriage gets better. You skip to work with happiness. Your whole life is something that others desire.

Surely you want the H Factor? What mentally sane person wouldn't want to live a life full of absolute, overwhelming, overflowing happiness? It's the best way to live. The British comedian Ken Dodd once wrote a song that went like this: "Happiness, happiness, the greatest gift that I possess. I thank the Lord that I possess more than my share of happiness." You can be singing the same song if you put the principles within this book into practice.

Happiness is...

So what does being happy actually mean? The dictionary defines happiness as feeling pleasure, satisfaction or joy. It's as simple as that but does take a bit of work. If you are not happy right now, it may take several months to start turning things around. Psychologists tell us that habits are formed when you do something at least twenty-one times. After practising the principles in this book on a regular basis and allowing them to change you as a person, happiness will be the by-product.

Aristotle, the famous philosopher, said thousands of years ago that happiness is an activity that requires skill and focus. It is not passive like relaxing in a bath. It requires effort. Aldous Huxley said that happiness is generally the by-product of other activities. So you need to be focused and determined. Regularly dip into the chapters of this book and review where you're at. Never give up. The prize is worth it.

Do you really want to be happy? Then you need to make getting the H Factor the focus of your life. Believe me, it is really there for the taking. If you're depressed, a bit miserable or just falling short of true happiness, this A to Z course in happiness is for you. It can revolutionise your daily life.

Trouble Still Happens

In case you are beginning to get worried about me, let me point out something important: the H Factor doesn't ignore life's problems. We'll be discussing that in a later chapter. Everyone has problems. They're a sign that you're alive!

But, the H Factor will teach you how to have overflowing happiness *despite* your problems. It will help you relish life and all that it throws at you. It will tackle all aspects of your life. It will improve your character. It will provide you with determination, encouragement and fun. Your health will improve. You'll make a mark on life. People will remember you fondly when you're gone. They'll be eager to be around you while you're alive.

The H Factor contains the secret of living. You'll know the meaning of life. You'll have all the armour to fight life and be victorious with a capital V. Do you really want it? I wrote this book out of a tragic realization that most people really aren't happy. Everyone wants to be happy, but they have a vague, aimless hope or wish, a hopeless stab in the dark at happiness, always falling short.

Born to Be Happy

People are generally born happy and face life with relish. Babies and toddlers enjoy everything they face. They love to play, laugh and take on challenges such as walking and talking. But that soon ends, usually by the time they leave school and often much earlier. They're beaten down by fears, insecurities and the negative things spoken over them. If their parents have divorced or have financial difficulties or argue then they very often end up hating life before hitting their teens. Sometimes this descends into thoughts of suicide. It really is a tragedy.

People often fill up their unhappy lives with whatever they can. Sometimes it's alcohol. Very often it's drugs, sex or even football, fitness or TV soaps! They don't want to face the reality of what is a painful daily journey through life with no prospect of a breakthrough. They very often end up dying sad and unhappy, or at the very least not having enjoyed life. They started off their life's journey full of enthusiasm, expectancy and energy, but ended it full of bitterness, resentment and regrets. They failed to enjoy the journey.

There really is another way. It's the way of the H Factor. Do you really, really want it? Be brutally honest with yourself. Pretending to yourself that you're happy won't get you anywhere. If you do, happiness will always escape you. Yes, you will get opposition. Some people will try to keep you down, to keep you unhappy. Maybe they won't like the new you. As you get happier and carry something of the H Factor around with you, they won't be happy with that! It will be a challenge to them. You'll start to realize who your friends really are. Your true friends will love to see you grow, to enjoy life, to be happy. Very often people keep themselves feeling good by being with others who are having a bad time. But that's not really living.

It's Decision Time!

Start right now by making a decision that you want the H Factor. Then resolve that you will go for the prize with everything you have. Read the chapters one at a time and make notes on them. Underline key phrases. Highlight them. Write nuggets of wisdom down and put them on your pc's screensaver, your bathroom mirror, your car dashboard. Put the ideas into practise and see your life change for the better. You'll be thrilled as you – and your friends and family – see the amazing changes.

I hope you've caught a bit about what the H Factor is all about. Now get yourself a coffee and settle back to find out more about this wonderful philosophy of living. The H Factor really is the best way to live.

Summary

1. Happy people are healthier and more successful in life
2. There is a prescription for happiness that is available to everyone
3. Problems will still happen, they are a part of life
4. You will need focus and determination to practise the principles in this book, but it will change your life
5. Make a decision now to learn how to be happy

The A Factor:
Attitude

"The greatest part of our happiness depends on our
dispositions, not our circumstances."

Henry Ford

You can choose to be happy. It's a choice. When you wake up
there's a decision to be made. Are you going to be happy or
unhappy? I always make the same choice. I choose to be
incredibly, ecstatically, deliriously happy. Period.

It sounds silly and simplistic – but it's true. It's called "attitude"
and it's crucially important to help you get the H Factor. An old
mentor of mine, Frank Houston from Australia, had a saying
that, "Everything is a matter of choice – a decision." He was
right. Your attitude determines so much in your life.

- Are you attracting the wrong sort of people?
  Then change your attitude.
- Are you lacking good friends?
  Then change your attitude.
- Are you failing to get a promotion in your job?
  Then change your attitude.

I could go on and on and on. Your attitude determines your
altitude. The better your attitude, the higher you can climb. A

good attitude opens doors of opportunity and relationships, but a bad attitude closes them. I've watched so many people flunk in life because of a "stinking" attitude. I've seen colleagues with huge potential and massive personalities lose in life because their attitude failed to live up to their talent.

> **A good attitude opens doors of opportunity and relationships, but a bad attitude closes them.**

Two people could live in the same town with the same life and job. Yet one person could be having the H Factor life while the other is miserable. The difference is their attitude to life. I recently heard of a lady called Margaret who was crippled with multiple sclerosis and riddled with cancer. She spent every day in a wheelchair but was one of the happiest people you'd ever meet. Her attitude was that there is always someone else worse off. What a fantastic attitude!

You Can Change Your Attitude

Attitude is about having a right mindset and the right thoughts. You may not want to get up at 5.30am to start work but you have to choose your response to your circumstances. So have you got the Attitude Factor? Are you a positive type of person who people want to be around or are you known as a "moaning old goat" who people want to stay away from? If you're the latter then don't fret. You can change your attitude. It may take a lot of work and be a slow process, but you can. You need to start practising the habits now that will eventually change your attitude. Remember that it takes just twenty-one repetitions of doing something to form a habit. Eventually you will *become* your habits. Here are some practical tips to point you on the way to the Attitude Factor.

Be Positive

The founder of the Ford motor company, Henry Ford, said, "If you think you can or you think you can't, either way you're right." So believe that you can. Face challenges with a positive "I can" attitude.

People often comment that if I fell in cow dung I'd come up smelling of roses. My attitude believes that great things will happen no matter what. That's why it's tragic that I meet so many miserable people who fail to live each day as positively as they can. They have got into the habit of being negative, and that's a hard habit to break. This sort of attitude leaves a bad atmosphere wherever they go.

As a Christian minister I believe with all my heart that the Bible is truth. It is what Almighty God has given us to help us live. It is alive and full of words to help us in all situations of our lives. And the Bible's words have amazing power. Try it. I find I can do anything through believing that Jesus Christ, the Son of God, is with me wherever I go. One line in the Bible says, *"I can do all things through Christ who strengthens me."* Believe that you can. With God's help you can do anything. Believe He is with you and helping you.

Act As If

Do you want to up your attitude? Then hear this simple but effective principle. It is three words: "Act As If". This technique was first described by psychology pioneer Professor William James and was continued by the great positive thinking writer Norman Vincent Peale. It is a powerful technique.

Until I put the power of these three words into my life I failed to get the H Factor. Oh yes, I was popular, my thoughts were okay. Life was pretty fine too. But these three simple words sent me soaring.

The technique goes like this. Act the way you want to be and soon enough you will become like you act. A self-image held in the mind becomes truth in the long run. About twenty years ago I began to realize that to ascend higher in my personal and professional life, I had to "Act As If" I was already where I wanted to be. So often, if I am down I will act as if I'm happy and I then I am! Similarly, for you it might be that you want to be happier. Then Act As If. You might want to more enthusiastic, or a more confident person or a better actor. Then Act As If. It really is as simple as that. That's attitude. The belief that you can do something – and in fact already are something – carries power. What are you waiting for?

Be Content

You also need to learn to be content. Contentment is a product of your attitude. No matter what you've been given in life, you can be content. It's a fact that someone broke, fat and facially challenged can be more content than a beautiful princess. Take the case of Lady Diana. If all the millions of words are to be believed, though she was beautiful, rich, radiant, personable, famous, kind and compassionate, the future Queen of England never had the H Factor. Yet she had everything the world seems to want.

> **Contentment is a product of your attitude.**
> **No matter what you've been given in life,**
> **you can be content.**

So many things try to take that level of contentment away. TV adverts tell us to get another job, a bigger house, a new kitchen, a better car, more expensive make-up – yet all these things cannot get you the H Factor.

If you're content with what you've got in life, you've taken a large step towards getting the H Factor. The worst thing you can ever do is wish you were someone else, or that you had your neighbour's wealth or body or face or husband. Be happy with what you've got. That doesn't mean settling for second best. You can set worthwhile goals to make your life better, but constant thoughts of wanting to be someone else are futile and destructive.

Summary

1. You can choose to be happy, it is all about attitude
2. Act As If and you will become what you want to become
3. Circumstances shouldn't dictate how happy you are
4. We all have the potential for happiness
5. Be positive all the time and be content with what you have

The B Factor: *Balance*

"Happiness is not a matter of intensity but of balance and
order and rhythm and harmony."

Thomas Merton

Balance should be a priority for your life. The whole world is in
perfect balance. God made it so. We live in world that exists in a
perfectly balanced mix of gases, chemicals and light to ensure
mankind's continued survival. We also have man and woman,
dark and light, hot and cold, wet and dry, Abbott and Costello![1]
The list goes on and on.

If you don't have balance in your life then eventually it will
catch up with you. All truth taken to extreme becomes error.
It's true, for instance, that God still does miracle healings today,
but if your whole faith is focused on this one thing then you'll
be out of balance and you can't have the H Factor.

I've got a mate who used to drink so much Coke that it made
him ill. It just isn't sensible to have, or focus on, too much of
one thing in life, whether it's food, drink, work or whatever.
Think of some other people you know who are out of balance.

[1] For anyone under the age of about thirty-five, Abbott and Costello were one
of the greatest comedy teams in show business, who had mastered the art of the
straightman/clown relationship!

They won't have overflowing happiness, H Factor style. They can't! I don't care whether they drink too much Coke, watch too much telly, run too many miles, read too much, talk too much or make too much money. It isn't healthy and they're out of balance.

Are you balanced? You need to be and you can be. To become balanced you need to examine your life and see how it shapes up. I believe there are five areas you need to work on in order to provide the right kind of balance for life. They are the areas of fun, family and friends, study, work, and the spiritual.

1. Fun

Fun. What a word! I love it! It's so important that I'll be coming back to it in a later chapter. It's crucial for overflowing happiness. Do you make time to socialise and to play a bit? Do you enjoy your holidays? I have a philosophy in my life that you will have heard before: work hard, play hard. And, oh boy, do I know how to play! For me fun means getting together with friends for a good belly laugh, enjoying a sauna or jacuzzi or watching a great film.

> **You were made to enjoy life.**
> **Write that truth down and stick it**
> **on your bathroom mirror.**

Here's a truth you perhaps don't yet realize: you were made to enjoy life. Write that truth down and stick it on your bathroom mirror. Say out loud: "I was made to enjoy life." It's true. Believe it. God didn't make you for a dull, boring life with no fun. Not a bit of it. He wants you to have fun and is delighted when you do.

Part of creating the recipe for fun in life means taking time to switch off. Our bodies need to rest from work. You'll probably know the saying, "All work and no play makes Jack a dull boy." Well, I'm saying that Jack needs to be liberated a bit and get his life back into balance! Jack certainly hasn't got the H Factor because he doesn't have the Fun Factor.

How do you have fun? For you it could be reading a book. It could be jogging, juggling or medieval jousting. It really doesn't matter what it is so long as you're enjoying it. If you're out of balance in this area then begin to change today. Write a chart on a piece of paper, listing the five areas down one side and ticking each area where you feel out of balance. Then down the other side of the paper write down what you plan to do to change.

2. Family and Friends

Are you neglecting your relationships? Are you out of balance in terms of the time you put in to your family and friendships? If so you're playing a dangerous game. It's an old cliché but no one lies on their deathbed wishing they'd spent more time in the office. It won't be a consideration for you either. You'll be thinking about those close to you and those you love. You'll be thinking about the special moments you've shared with them.

Very often we are sold the lie that having "things" will make us happy. They won't. They cannot. They'll give us a temporary "high" that will fade in days, weeks or months. That isn't happiness. It's your relationships with your family and friends that count. It is extremely difficult to have the H Factor if you've got no friends. I've got loads of friends and know how important they are.

Someone once said to me: "If you can find one true friend in your lifetime then you're a rich person." That makes me a multi-millionaire! Think for a moment. What are your relationships like? Do you enjoy being with your friends and family? Do they enjoy being with you? Have you got some close relationships? If the answer to these questions is no then you've got some work to do. And remember, to have friends you need to be friendly!

> **Those who never listen and never ask other people about themselves can't have the H Factor.**

Perhaps all round you need to become more of the sort of person that people like. Selfish people don't have real friends. Those who never listen and never ask other people about themselves can't have the H Factor. Does this describe you? You won't be liked by others – and ultimately you can't be happy by focusing on yourself.

3. Study

Are you still learning or do you think you know it all? There is nothing worse than someone so puffed up with pride that they can't learn new things. That's arrogance. Leaders are learners. So are those who have the H Factor. You need to make time for study as part of having a balanced life. We have incredible minds, yet scientists tell us we only use up to about 7 percent of our mind's capacity. Learning new things will help keep your mind active, help it to grow and make you a more interesting person. If you're stagnating in your brain capacity then you'll fail to fully develop in a social capacity and lack the wellbeing that this brings. You may have been promoted at work but if you don't learn new things then you'll probably not get much further. This brings us nicely on to . . .

4. Work

Are you obsessed with work? Then you could be a bore. You're also in danger of getting burnt out. I've seen it so often in friends and colleagues. Relationships suffer. Health suffers.

Of course, work is crucial for our mental wellbeing – and we need it to get the H Factor. But doing crazy hours and not being balanced in other areas in life is a danger sign. If you find that you're working seven days a week or doing eighty hours work each week without some form of relaxation or switch-off time, then you're out of balance. Burnout does no one any good.

See sense before you seize up. Don't believe the lie that work is the be all and end all. It's not. It's a means to an end. Like I said earlier, it is relationships that win the day – every time. So work at them. You only need so much money, so what or who are you working for? Your friends and family want to see more of you, not your money. If you die tomorrow then what has it all been for? (We'll discover more about finding your purpose in a few chapters time!)

5. The Spiritual Dimension

Do you believe in a Creator of the Universe? Do you believe in a God who is interested in you, who loves you?

The spiritual dimension is of vital importance as you aim for that elusive H Factor. You can have all the other areas in balance – fun, family and friends, study, work – and still be out of balance.

We are not only flesh and blood. Life is not only about the material items we have. There is a whole world that we cannot see with our eyes. God put a desire within every human He created to want to worship something. We can worship whatever we like, be it a soccer team, our wife or husband, a film star or something as simple as the sun or the moon. The choice is up to us. But my belief is that we have an empty space within us that can only be filled by Almighty God.

As part of getting a balanced life, do you need to think more about seeking a spiritual dimension to your life? This is not about me ramming my beliefs down your throat. Your journey in life will be different from mine, but you need a spiritual experience, something that is not found in material things . . . a real purpose to live for.

Summary

1. Be balanced in all areas of your life
2. Make time for fun, family and friends, study, work and the spiritual

The C Factor:
Character

> "Character is like a tree and reputation like its shadow. The shadow is what we think of it; the tree is the real thing."
>
> Abraham Lincoln

Your character is who you are when no one can see you. You can't invest in a more valuable asset in life than your character. No one can rob you of it and it's the only thing we take with us when we die. It's more precious than solid gold and cheaper than a new Mercedes Benz, but to be developed correctly it does require some effort.

How do you react if you're criticised? Are you loyal, trustworthy, honest, positive and able to empathise with others? Or are you negative, back-stabbing and selfish? That's your character. It's seen in what we do in private, how we live, where we go, who our friends are, and particularly in our motives for what we do and don't do.

Being Outweighs Doing

What we are is far more important than what we do. "Being" outweighs "Doing". If we have a bad character then life will eventually come crashing down around us.

> **What we are is far more important than what we do.
> "Being" outweighs "doing".**

The best-selling author, Jeffrey Archer, is one of the most incredibly talented and resilient characters to have lived in the last fifty years. He reached the top of politics, writing and journalism. His attitude was fantastic in one sense. His determination (see the D Factor) was even better. He managed to become a millionaire and had career success despite humble beginnings. Then he lost it all, but made a success again! But during his life he got caught up in a web of lies revealing huge flaws in his character. He went to prison for perjury but came back again to achieve success. The truth is: character is far better than talent.

When Jesus, the Son of God, wrote the Sermon on the Mount (see Matthew chapter 5 in the Bible) it wasn't all about rules and regulations like his opponents the Pharisees taught, but about character. You see, character always comes before conduct. (In fact, while we're on the subject, the Beatitudes featured in Matthew 5 have been known as the "Be Happy Attitudes"! Read them and see.)

Hollywood

Why is character so important for the H Factor? Because happiness depends on who we are and not just what we do. I've watched so many people's lives collapse because their character was chaotic. Some people reach the top of their profession only to be let down by a flawed character. Hollywood is littered with stories of "stars" whose lack of good character was their own worst enemy. They had fame, fortune, fans by the bucket-load, and a future as bright as the California sun. Yet, they had anything but the H Factor. Their bad character toppled them from their perch. Bad character is a fast-track route to misery. Sometimes the arrogant, the manipulative bully, the cheat and the fraud may soar to the top. They certainly have the X Factor and seem to have the H Factor. But it's a matter of time before their character causes a crushing downfall. I don't believe that you can be hilariously happy if you're sensationally selfish. I don't believe you can have the H Factor if you secretly cheat those around you; if you bully or manipulate others. Integrity is essential to real happiness.

Inbuilt Sensor

It is also true that if you are secretly doing the wrong things or thinking wrong thoughts your conscience will be flashing "red alert". You have an inbuilt sensor that will tell you when you're doing wrong things. The Bible calls it sin. Sometimes this can lead to guilt. Thankfully, we can get rid of this (see the X Factor). On top of sin is usually the worry that what we are secretly doing wrong will eventually come to light. Fear and worry are the enemies of the H Factor.

Now, don't misunderstand me. I'm not pointing the finger. We're all flawed human beings. We all are nothing when compared to the character of a perfect God. So none of us can point our finger at others without three pointing back at us. I continually have to work on my character and fail in many areas. What I'm saying is that we all need to be constantly assessing our character. We need to be brutally honest with ourselves. There's nothing more futile than lying to ourselves.

Make a Decision

If you're constantly lying then resolve to stop lying. If you're a cheat then stop cheating. If you're secretly seething and jealous when someone is successful then practise being happy for them. It's a choice. You can choose to stay with the same old character traits or you can vow to be different, to improve your character.

How much do you want the H Factor? Then resolve to improve your character. It's not going to get you instant success, but will help you win through in the long run. You might not win a million pounds or dollars, secure a powerful job or become an overnight magnet to members of the opposite sex. But you will be pleasing God and building a foundation for long-term happiness.

> **The phrase "birds of a feather flock together" is very true. If you mix with people with bad habits, you'll start to pick the habits up too. Start to change your social scene.**

Who are you mixing with? The Bible tells us that *"bad company corrupts good character"* (1 Corinthians 15:33 NIV). The phrase "birds of a feather flock together" is very true. If you mix with people with bad habits, you'll start to pick the habits up too. Start to change your social scene. If someone is obviously heading down the wrong path, watch how long you spend with them.

Take the Character Test

Below are a few important aspects of your character. Take a few minutes to mentally assess where you are and if you admit you're lacking, then vow to take measures to improve. Rate yourself from 1 meaning totally true, to 10, not true at all. Be totally honest with yourself. You can't improve if you don't know where you stand.

- I'm tolerant of others
- I'm selfless
- I'm faithful
- I'm loyal
- I always tell the truth
- I react to criticism well
- I control my temper
- I celebrate people's successes

Summary

1. Character is who you are when no one can see you
2. We all need to constantly assess elements of our character
3. Consciously make a decision to improve your character
4. You become like the people you spend time with

The D Factor:
Determination

"The man who can drive himself further
once the effort gets painful is the man who will win."
Sir Roger Bannister (first runner to break the four-minute mile)

Call it what you like – grit, fight or the never-give-up spirit –
you need determination to get the H Factor. If you wilt, give
up too early or collapse under pressure then you can never
have overflowing happiness. Nothing worthwhile was ever
achieved by someone who gave up at the first opportunity.
Those with overflowing happiness never quit – whatever the
obstacles.

> **Having a "never give up" mentality is crucial
> in all areas of your life.**

One of my heroes, British wartime Prime Minister Winston
Churchill, had the Determination Factor. He led Britain to
stand alone against the evil plans of Adolf Hitler to take over the
world. He never quit even when it started to look a bit bleak.
Years later he gave a memorable speech to college students in
which he gave some valuable life advice. He said: "Never ever,

ever, ever give up." He was right. Get the fighting spirit within you. Never quit. Never give up. Fight to the finish. That's determination. Dogged determination.

Never Give Up

Having a "never give up" mentality is crucial in all areas of your life. What have you thought about giving up lately? A difficult job where you're getting opposition or something you know is really worthwhile, a friendship, a marriage? Many worthwhile things would never have been achieved if certain people had given up too soon – and people have overcome some remarkable obstacles to achieve amazing things. Children's author Enid Blyton overcame hundreds of rejection slips for her stories before getting her first book published. She went on to see dozens of fantastic novels published that have influenced generations of children. Thomas Edison would never have invented the electric light if he'd allowed years of failed attempts at doing so to stop him.

Genius Is One Percent Inspiration

Edison had a saying that "genius is one percent inspiration and 99 percent perspiration." He knew that worthwhile, world-changing projects took grit, fight and dogged determination. Edison had the Determination Factor. The only time that success comes before work is in the dictionary!

When I was a toned and fit young man (that seems a long time ago!) I used to do cross-country running. Boy, was that tough. Every single muscle in my body would groan under the strain as I pounded the last few hundred yards to collapse and win a personal victory. My sweat brought about success. There's no joy in giving up on a marathon after a mile.

So how do you get this fighting spirit? It's simple. Resolve never to quit. Never give up. There has to be something within you that knows you'll never stop. Sometimes you may think about quitting, but develop that steel within you that knows you'll never lose the fight. Vitally important is keeping your eyes on the goal. Don't let discouragement rob you. Others may not have the same vision or goal as you, so know what it is you want and go for it with gusto! The Bible tells us that David encouraged himself in the Lord (1 Samuel 30:6). How often I've had to keep this personal discipline, but it always pays great dividends.

> **Sometimes you may think about quitting, but develop that steel within you that knows you'll never lose the fight.**

Be Determined to Be Happy

Did you know that you can actually determine yourself to be happy? Happiness will come as a by-product of putting this book's principles into practice, but you can set happiness as your goal and never give up.

So often you hear people say that perhaps they were never destined to be happy. Rubbish! Happiness is there for everyone. What a waste if you go through life and never experience it to the full. That overflowing happiness would make your life's journey so much better. To get this happiness – the H Factor – you need to resolve to get it. Set it as your goal. Know within that you'll never quit until you get it. Remember that you'll need the 99 percent perspiration that Edison talked about. You'll need the fighting spirit of Churchill. Never let rejection slips stop the pursuit of your goal. It's an attitude of mind. Look at yourself in the mirror and tell yourself you'll never quit. Write it down and pin it in a prominent position so it can act as a reminder.

Goals for Happiness

One quick point. Our "forgetories" tend to be better than our memories, which is why you'll need to re-read this A to Z prescription for happiness on a regular basis. Then you'll need to keep a journal and write things down. You'll also have to pin things up where you can see them each day.

> **Settling for the comfortable, non-exerting status quo is not an option for the man or woman who wants the H Factor.**
> **Set your goals and write them down.**

What goals do you need to set in order get the H Factor? Well, they need to be worthwhile ones. You may not be inventing the electric light, publishing a world-changing novel or even fighting an evil enemy, but your goals still need to be worthwhile. If you want to make a million so you can live it up, buy yourself booze, drugs and holidays, then that won't get you the H Factor. But making a million to create projects to help disadvantaged children would. So would using money to secretly "bless" other people with gifts. So would giving the money away to the poor across the world. They're H Factor-type goals – not selfish, pleasure-seeking goals to please no one but yourself. Perhaps you're determined to complete that college course, to win promotion at work or to get your kids a good education. Great!

Don't Settle for the Status Quo

Settling for the comfortable, non-exerting status quo is not an option for the man or woman who wants the H Factor. Set your goals and write them down. Have an ultimate dream you want to achieve, then make one-, three- and five-year goals to help you achieve them. Think of balancing the areas of your life in the setting of your worthwhile goals. Be sure you have the skills and abilities to achieve them. Then go for them. Let nothing stop you. Never give up.

Summary

1. You need determination to get the H Factor
2. You can achieve amazing things if you're a fighter
3. Be determined to be happy
4. Set worthwhile goals
5. Never, ever, ever give up!

The E Factor:
Encouragement

"No one can be happy without a friend,
nor be sure of his friend till he is unhappy."
Thomas Fuller (seventeenth-century British physician)

"Let us be grateful to people who make us happy. They are
the charming gardeners who make our souls blossom."
Marcel Proust (nineteenth-century French intellectual)

"But encourage one another daily..."
The Bible (Hebrews 3:13 NIV)

Don't underestimate the power of encouragement. It's one of
the most wonderful things in the whole world anyone can give
to another person and we all need to receive it. This word
doesn't sound very exciting but it's central to the H Factor. It is
a word that is easily taken apart. The prefix *en* is from the Greek
and means "full of". The next part, "courage", is taken from
the word *coeur* which means "heart" or "strength". Literally, it
means that a person who has a full amount of courage inside
them is achieving a higher state of mental and emotional
wellbeing than a discouraged person. Are you an encourager or
a discourager?

> **If you aim to be an encourager you can spread happiness within your social circle. If you're a discourager then you'll destroy dreams, prevent potential and kill creativity.**

We All Need Encouragement

For every Paul there has to be a Barnabas.[2] Who's encouraging you? Who are you encouraging? You can either be a positive help to those around you or you can be a hindrance. Which are you going to be? If you aim to be an encourager you can spread happiness within your social circle. If you're a discourager then you'll destroy dreams, prevent potential and kill creativity. You see, Eddie Encourager draws people to him. He is the sort of person who people like. In contrast, people avoid Davie Discourager like the plague.

Remember that the H Factor is about living life to the max, not only for you but for those around you. What better way to do that than to encourage yourself – and others – to pursue so-called impossible dreams?

I wouldn't be the sort of person I am today if I hadn't had encouraging people around me. My mum and dad were great. So are my wife and friends and family. I've also had to learn to encourage myself.

Who are your encouragers? Who are you encouraging?

At what point do we stop being encouraging to people? Only a cruel bully would discourage a baby from learning to walk,

---

[2] Barnabas often travelled with the Apostle Paul, writer of most of the New Testament. His real name was actually Joseph, but the other apostles dubbed him "Barnabas" which literally means "son of encouragement", because that's what he kept on doing!

talk and read. We all marvel at the wonder of a new life and we want to see children rise to new levels as they discover the world around them. We encourage them to take their first steps and walk. We encourage their first words and we encourage them to write, paint and skip. Yet so often these mega confident pre-schoolers are turned into bumbling wrecks afraid to take on any new challenge. The discouraging comments of parents, teachers and pupils leave them uninspired. That's why encouragers are so vital. They help inspire dreams. They help people to achieve their goals and help create happiness in the lives of others.

Don't Be a Discourager

There's no point having Davie Discourager in your life. Your life's journey is tough enough without discouragement. Get him or her out of your life. You can do without them! Furthermore, if you are the Davie Discourager then grow up and get a grip. With a personality like that you can never have the H Factor. Davie can never be a truly happy person. The H Factor eludes him and always will.

Why is Davie Discourager like he is? Well it certainly isn't because he is happy. On the contrary, he is deeply unhappy on the inside. He is possibly full of resentment, bitterness and even hatred. He possibly hates himself and wishes he is something he isn't. He resents other people being happy. He is bitter about others being successful and enjoying life. He lives in a dark bubble of bitterness and he takes a morbid satisfaction in the failures of others, which temporarily makes him feel better about himself. He is cripplingly insecure.

If this is you then be brutally honest with yourself and determine to be different. Maybe you need to spend several months of self-reflection to see why you are like you are.

Prayerfully seek to change. Ask God and He will help you. If you don't, not only will the H Factor elude you, but you'll repel others. No one wants to be around discouraging types. Ask yourself what contribution you are making to the lives of others.

Be an Encourager

Instead, resolve to be an Eddie Encourager. Eddie is like a beacon of light, spreading encouragement wherever he goes. People want him around. He releases people to be the very best they can be. He recognises that everyone has talent and that it is a dreadful waste for it not to be used. Eddie wants the best for everyone.

> **There's nothing greater than seeing people helped by encouragement. An encouraging word can achieve so much. And everyone – even the most optimistic person you know – needs encouraging.**

There's little bitterness or insecurity in Eddie. He actually celebrates when others reach their potential. If he succeeds himself his first thought is how to lift up others. He puts others first, before himself. Eddie is well on the way to the H Factor. He has discovered a wonderful secret: that enjoying life is not all about buying nice things and getting big promotions. It is about thinking of others. It is about being positive in all situations.

There's nothing greater than seeing people helped by encouragement. An encouraging word can achieve so much. And everyone – even the most optimistic person you know – needs encouraging. Who's encouraging the local head teacher who is positively influencing the lives of thousands of children? Who's encouraging the woman who helps run the local soup kitchen for the homeless? Who's encouraging your country's president or prime minister? Believe me, someone needs to. They will achieve far more and enjoy their work if you do. Why don't you seek to encourage at least one person before today ends. Better still, seek to make this a daily practice. Every day find one person you can encourage to fulfil their dreams. This could be your husband or wife, your children, your friend, your neighbour, your boss or your work colleague, the local post-man or your child's teacher.

So many people shrink from life. They fail to achieve what God wants for them because they don't believe in themselves. Perhaps a bully or a parent verbally abused them and told them they were no good. Maybe teachers or classmates or a boss told them they'd never make it. It could even have been an abusive spouse. Whatever the reason, they have now believed the lie that they amount to nothing. They don't know the potential they have so they fail to even have a go. They feel worthless. It is a sad and pathetic waste.

I've seen people's whole countenance change as a result of being encouraged. Their levels of faith rise and goals and dreams are rekindled. Don't underestimate this truth. As you encourage others **you** become the recipient of happiness. If you will encourage others to overcome their own worry habit, you will get greater power over it yourself, and you will shed warmth over a discouraged and bewildered world. It is far better to give than receive. It's an H Factor principle to think of others rather than yourself.

Encouragers are in short supply. That's why so few people have the H Factor. You can make a huge difference in the world by encouraging wherever you go. Look for the best in others. Look for a gift in others and nurture it.

You've got to remember though that it's important not to be encouraging people to seek stuff that just isn't good for them. That's encouragement in a negative fashion. It's like someone encouraging me to be a fashion model or a pop singer. It just isn't going to happen! Encourage others into areas where you can see they were made to go.

But resolve to do this: don't leave life to the Davie Discourager characters. Instead, let the Eddie Encourager within you rise to the surface. The Bible tells us to *"encourage one another"* (1 Thessalonians 5:11).

Summary

1. Encouragement is vital in life, everyone needs it
2. Don't be a discourager, others won't want to be around you
3. Be an encourager, it will make you happy

The F Factor:
Fun

"A sense of humour is good for you. Have you ever heard of
a laughing hyena with heartburn?"
Bob Hope (British-born actor and comedian)

*"A cheerful heart is good medicine,
but a broken spirit saps a person's strength"*
The Bible (Proverbs 17:22 NLT)

The Bible says that laughter is a good medicine – and indeed it is! I believe in fun wholeheartedly and so does God. You cannot have the H Factor without the Fun Factor. There's little point living this life as miserable as sin. Enjoy life. Have some fun. Laugh a lot! You can either enjoy your journey in life or you can just cope with it. Or you can even hate it.

There's no better way of living life than by having fun. Work hard, play hard is the best way to go. So when you play, make sure you're having fun. I have fun wherever I go and whatever I do. I know I'm a Christian but I'd have enjoyed the other life as well. That's just the way I am. If you're a misery then you'll repel people. Those who love fun are great to be around. They have the H Factor.

You need to live life like a child would do. Children are amazing. They get excited about new things. They play. They have fun. They laugh an incredible amount. In fact, children laugh about 150 times a day on average. Adults laugh about four or five times a day on average. What does that tell you? That people lose the ability to have fun once they get past childhood. That's terrible. Take a health check right now on your Fun Factor level. Do people want to be around you? Do you cheer people up? Do you manage to have a laugh even through difficult times?

> **You need to live life like a child would do.**
> **Children are amazing. They get excited about**
> **new things. They play. They have fun.**
> **They laugh an incredible amount.**

We can look back and laugh at all sorts of things. Once I went on a Christian missions trip with a friend and stayed in the home of a young married couple we had barely met. Me being a bit of a joker I thought I'd play a practical joke on my friend. After he had gone to bed I spontaneously planned to enter his room and jump on top of him, which I did. I leapt from the floor shouting "Batman fatman" in an attempt to smother him while asleep. However, it was only when I was flying through the air in my boxer shorts that I realized the person in the bed was a semi-naked woman – the young married lady we were staying with! I had got the wrong room! Meanwhile her husband watched the unfolding drama while shaving in the bathroom!

On another occasion I bought some gel from a joke shop that promised to solidify cups of tea. I put the gel into a cup of tea at a party and went to throw it at a woman I barely knew. Sadly the gel didn't work and instead the tea saturated her lovely new dress! Staggeringly embarrassing at the time, but funny to look back on! It's good to see the funny side of incidents.

Work Can Be Fun

One of the most inspiring places I've heard of in recent years is a humble fish market in Seattle, America. Some boss there wanted to make his fish market famous so he changed the working philosophy that his staff had. Now it is a place of fun. Those who sell the fish just have a great laugh. They make their work fun. They make it fun for shoppers. They regularly get crowds watching as they do silly things like throwing and catching fish, and it brings them great business. I saw this place on an amazingly motivational DVD called, simply, "Fish"!

They believe in a fourfold model of creating a great business. These are:

1. Have fun
2. Be there for people
3. Make the people's day
4. Choose your attitude

They believe that if you can have fun in your business then you will attract more business, and it works! Not only does having fun attract more people to you, it also makes you more content and happy as well. The Fish DVD encourages you to make people's day and to choose your attitude as part of a motivational "fishing" philosophy. I'd heartily recommend all of these things as great tips along the way to getting the H Factor.

Are you having fun in your work? If you're not then you can do one of two things. You can change your attitude to start having fun, or you can leave – after seeking the will of God first, of course! You spend a huge proportion of your waking life involved in work so it's vital that you enjoy it. Remember back to chapter 1. You need to change your attitude by acting as if you already have the thing you want. In this case you need to act as if your job is fun. If you start having fun your job will change dramatically! You'll enrich your life and you're boss won't think you're the same person! (If you're a boss then spread a fun attitude all across your firm and you'll stop your workers leaving!)

> **Are you having fun in your work? …**
> **You spend a huge proportion of your waking**
> **life involved in work so it's vital**
> **that you enjoy it.**

If you really can't get on with the job. If you hate the boss and he or she hates you and you sit looking at the clock all day, then perhaps it's time to find a new job. But, before you do, be careful to examine your motivation and make sure it's not your own bad attitude at fault. If it is, then getting a new job won't change anything. Find your skills and use them. Life is really too short not to enjoy it!

Have Fun – Change Your Marriage

You also need fun in your marriage. You need to create this as a priority. This is one thing I urge everyone to do. Divorce is so incredibly painful for all concerned, the man, the woman, the children, friends and family. There are no winners in divorce. God really did intend for marriage to be "till death do us part" and that's the way it should be. So how do you get fun in your marriage? Here's a three-point plan.

1. Forgive each other daily.
2. Make love to your partner twenty-four hours a day! By this I mean that you should wine and dine them, make them a cup of tea to start the day, think in terms of their interests, listen, love them, buy them little gifts, speak good things over them – and watch the fireworks fly that night!
3. Talk constantly and laugh about everything together. Communication is the key.

My wife Andrene once put cut-out red hearts everywhere, in my Bible, in my clothes, even in my shoes, just to demonstrate her love for me. I'm still finding them!

Similarly, you can help to build a fun atmosphere among your friends and associates. Once I put Olbas Oil into the boxer shorts of a great friend, Danny Guglielmucci, before he went into the sauna. The effect was to cause immense heat on the skin and incredible amusement . . . except for my pal of course! I've done other funny things such as wearing silly masks, making crank phone calls to friends and regularly telling jokes, all to lighten the atmosphere and make things fun.

I can't tell you how important fun is for you to enjoy life. In John 10:10 of the Bible it says that Jesus came so you could have life to the full. Having fun is part of this. I'm sure that Jesus enjoyed Himself and had fun with the disciples. He wants you and me to have the same.

I meet so many people who think you have to be straight-faced and miserable, so serious about everything. Not at all! Have fun! Don't let the misery mongers get you down. This life is for enjoying! The Fun Factor will launch you into a fun new future.

Summary

1. Enjoy your life, have fun, laugh more
2. Choose to have a fun attitude at work
3. Make your marriage fun
4. Have fun, be there for people, make people's day, choose your attitude
5. Laugh lots!

The G Factor:
Generosity

"Make all you can, save all you can, give all you can."
John Wesley (eighteenth-century Methodist preacher)

"We make a living by what we get,
we make a life by what we give."
Sir Winston Churchill (1874–1965)

"Each man should give what he has decided in his heart
to give, not reluctantly or under compulsion,
for God loves a cheerful giver."
The Bible (2 Corinthians 9:7 NIV)

Givers get the H Factor. Your level of generosity will determine your level of happiness! It's a universal law that you will be happier the more you give. If all you do is wait to get things then you'll never achieve the level of happiness you crave. How do I know that? Well, I live it. I believe passionately that giving is the best way to live. Have you ever had that "rosy glow" when you've given to charity? Imagine living that way all the time!

It may sound crazy to some to suggest that being a giver is the best way to do things, because the world seems to think you can, "buy your way to happiness". It says, if you buy this car or that house or that PC you will get even happier. But it's a lie.

Be a Cheerful Giver

The principle that giving leads to happiness is confirmed by God Himself who says in the Bible that, *"It is more blessed to give than receive"* (Acts 20:35 NKJV). The Bible also says that, *"God loves a cheerful giver."* And He does. Actually, He loves a non-cheerful one as well . . . but that's another story!

> **Do you live to give? Are you always looking for an opportunity to give what you have? Or do you wait to receive from others?**

So check now where you're at. Do you live to give? Are you always looking for an opportunity to give what you have? Or do you wait to receive from others? Be ruthlessly honest with yourself. Those who seek to keep what they have, rather than sharing, can never have the H Factor. That's a hard truth, but a truth nevertheless.

If you fail to give you'll never have any true friends. No one wants to be with a miser. If you live for yourself you'll forever fail to find true happiness. Not giving is a sign of an immature personality. Toddlers very often fail to share their toys with other children. They wait to be fed, changed and put to bed. Yes, they often make us laugh, but they don't think of other's needs or interests. They have to be taught to do that.

That's just what this chapter is all about. I want you to learn this privilege of giving because I so desperately want you to get the H Factor and be happy. Jesus came so we could have life to the full, overflowing and definitely above the average. That's how your life can be. It really can. You can be so happy you don't know what to do. So give a kick-start to your quest for happiness today. I learnt this principle very early on in my life but, still, I realize the level of happiness I get when I give even more.

Get the Giving Habit

Jesus talked a lot about giving. As God He knew how important it was to have a generous spirit. God's Word, the Bible, also teaches us about giving our tithes and offerings. God requests of us that we give the first part of our income back to Him. It represents the fact that we put Him first in our life. The Bible suggests a minimum of 10 percent of our income, but to get overflowing happiness start to give more.

> **Do you have too tight a grip on your possessions?**
> **Then let go of them. You were born with nothing**
> **and you will die with nothing.**
> **You can't take anything with you.**

It doesn't matter how much you give, but you need to realize that your money isn't really yours at all. Do you have too tight a grip on your possessions? Then let go of them. You were born with nothing and you will die with nothing. You can't take anything with you.

Start to build up a fund from which you can give to others. Perhaps you could sponsor a family in Africa. Maybe you could secretly give money or a food parcel to a struggling single mother on your road or regularly give to a worthy cause or charity. Become an eager giver in your world. See opportunities to give to others, whether it's your time, talents or money.

Before long you will be a habitual giver. What a great habit to have! You will start to be a giver beyond the norm. You will be far further down the road to getting the H Factor.

Be Wise with Your Money

Please be aware that I'm not talking about giving so that you get into debt. That's not what it is all about. Perhaps you have debts and money issues in your life. Foolish giving is not what it's all about. If you are in debt then you need to deal with it. Are you spending too much on material items? Then cut them out. Do you have credit cards? Then chop them up. You need to write a budget and stick to it. Find out where your finance is going wrong and be ruthless in sorting it out. If you're in serious debt you can't have the H Factor.

Rob Parsons has written an excellent book called *The Money Secret*[3] in which he advises on budgeting. I recommend you get a copy. It's also good to save for a rainy day. But the best way to secure more money in the long term is to give, give, give! How do I know that? Well, again it is by living it out in my own life and, more importantly, the Bible confirms that it's true. It says that whatever you sow you will also reap. It is what is known as a universal law and it works for everyone whether Christian or not yet Christian. If you give lots you will get even more. Whatever you give away will come back to you several times over.

God says that if you give the first part of your income to Him by giving it to your local church, He will open the windows of heaven and pour you out a blessing so big there will not be enough room to receive it (Malachi 3:10). What a promise that is! I've seen it work in my own life and in the lives of others who have discovered this secret.

---

[3]   Rob Parsons, *The Money Secret*, Hodder & Stoughton Ltd, 2005.

The famous author John Grisham reportedly gives 90 percent of his income away. He's discovered the secret of giving. Have you? We are never more like our Heavenly Father, God, than when we are giving. In John 3:16 the Bible explains that because God so loved the world He gave away His only Son Jesus Christ, so that people who believe in Him can live forever. What gigantic, gargantuan generosity!

Twice in my life I've felt to give away brand new cars that I've owned. I've tried to out-give a God whose very nature is giving ... it can't be done! Try it. There is a special feeling associated with giving that is far better than getting.

Summary

1. Getting things does not lead to happiness, but giving does
2. Grow up and learn how to "live to give"
3. Learn how to budget and to get out of debt
4. You reap what you sow. Give and you will receive
5. You can't out-give God!

The I Factor:
Inner Peace

*"The mind of sinful man is death, but the mind controlled
by the Spirit is life and peace."*
The Bible (Romans 8:6 NIV)

*"Peace I leave with you; my peace I give you.
I do not give to you as the world gives. Do not let your
hearts be troubled and do not be afraid."*
The Bible (John 14:27 NIV)

"First keep the peace within yourself,
then you can also bring peace to others."
Thomas à Kempis (1380–1471)

If there is one thing that people today have lost, it is their inner
peace. We swallow more "peace pills" now than ever before.
People seek peace through yoga, meditation, alcohol, deep
breathing, herbal quick fixes, saunas, massages, beta-blockers
and gardening! Not that many of these things are wrong ... but
they don't give lasting peace.

One hundred years ago peace was far more common.
Though there were world wars and poverty there were fewer
fractured families, less stress at work, more physical exercise
taking place and better networks of relationships. Now, people

are sprinting through the "rat race", trying to find time for friends and family whilst chasing crazy hours at work. There is little time for relaxation and very often, this kind of lifestyle leaves people drained and scarred emotionally.

> **People who are driven and who live life at a relentless pace often have to cope with wrecked relationships in later life.**

People who are driven and who live life at a relentless pace often have to cope with wrecked relationships in later life and have very little by way of a relational network to offer them support. The result is inner turmoil which can lead to alcoholism, drug abuse, sex addictions, self-harm and suicide – all of which have soared in recent years. No wonder books, magazines and New Age religions offering quick fixes for inner peace are so popular.

Do You Have It?

Do you have inner peace? Sit still for a moment. Put down this book, shut your eyes and see what thoughts run through your head. Are they positive thoughts of peace, hope, love and self-worth? Or are they thoughts of anxiety, worry, hatred and self-loathing? If you're in this latter category then you need to do some work before you can get overflowing happiness in your life. To get the H Factor you need to have inner peace.

How do you get it? Well, first find out why you have no peace. If you had a difficult childhood it could be responsible for the thoughts and feelings you have now. Perhaps you had alcoholic parents who abused you. Maybe you were bullied at school or weren't shown any love by anyone. Now you're older these things come back to haunt you. All those thoughts and feelings never leave you. If you've done nothing to alter your thought patterns or to receive healing for your past then these feelings will still be buried deep. They need slowly bringing to the surface and thinking through. If you find out why you have a lack of inner peace then you're half way to solving it. Pinpoint the source.

It's a tragedy when people suffering from inner turmoil cover up the problem by turning to drugs or alcohol to numb the pain. Every day they turn back to the bottle because they can't face who they really are. Perhaps they have guilt, shame or fear and don't know why. Whisky makes them feel better so they drink more and more, and become more and more dependent.

A guy I know called Marvin had terrible feelings of rejection as a teenager, caused by his parents' painful divorce and a messed-up family life and childhood. These experiences stayed with him as a young adult and he had little self-esteem. Marvin directed his life's focus towards alcohol, sex, hypnosis, meditation, education, football and anything else in a bid to get rid of the pain, guilt and shame that was wrecking his life. Eventually, staring suicide in the face, he cried out in desperation to God. "If You are there, then come into my life!" he urged, "otherwise, I'll kill myself because what's the point?" Marvin then began a period of self-discovery, realizing for the first time just what was causing his pain. With God to talk to as his guide and his healer, just a few years later Marvin is now fantastically happy. He is married and enjoying a great life living for others. He has the H Factor. So can you.

Take a Look at Your Life

Write down a journal of self-discovery to analyse your past. What has happened in your past? Perhaps one year your mum died or you failed your exams at school or were bullied. Write that down. Become more aware of your life and what might have caused your inner turmoil. Now relive some of the incidents and write down the feelings you had at the time. Was it hate, anger, shame? This may take several weeks to do but is very worthwhile. In the next stage you need to offer up these experiences to Jesus to put His healing touch on to them.

The Prince of Peace

Peace is not found in a pill, or drink or drugs. It is found through God. In the Bible, Jesus is called the "Prince of peace". He can heal all your hurts if you ask Him. Jesus is God. He created you and knows you intimately. He knows every incident, every hurt and every feeling you have. If you ask Him, He will totally heal your emotions. Try it. Say, "Lord God, please make me emotionally healthy and give me inner peace." Now believe it.

Jesus is the same yesterday, today and forever. It is nothing for Him to go back to your past. Imagine Him there in every incident in your life, holding your hand and healing your emotions. He will!

Jesus is the source of true peace. Invite Him into your life and He will start to help in every area. He can take your dependency off alcohol, drugs, sex, football or whatever else you're hooked on. God has provided His Bible for you to meditate on. The Bible has incredible power because its author is none other than Almighty God. When you read it you are tapping into His wonderful love and it is full of promises that will help you supernaturally to gain inner peace.

Speak Peace for Yourself

Try saying some of these phrases from the Bible and let them embed themselves into your subconscious: *"Peace be with you."*

"Be still, and know that I am God." Also try Psalm 23:2–3 which says, *"He leads me beside the still waters. He restores my soul."* *"He will keep him in perfect peace whose mind is focused on him."* As you speak out scriptures like these something supernatural will happen within you. The Bible helps you get in tune with the Creator. His Word is powerful and has much to help you.

I was aged only fourteen when I invited Jesus into my life. It was a wonderful feeling. I've never looked back. Inner peace has filled my life even through the difficult parts of life, the strains and the struggles which we all have. Even at the time of my mum's death I felt incredible pain and loss, yet there was the peace that comes from God. An artist once drew a picture of a storm that was raging. In the middle of the storm was a tiny bird in a small nest in a tree, totally protected and at peace. That is how we can be living when we have Almighty God as our companion, driving our life.

I really have to be honest with you and caution you against pursuing the world's "prescriptions" for inner peace. Many of them are false. The only true and worthwhile cure is Jesus Christ who can do miracles. Take it from me and tens of millions of others, Jesus really is the real thing. If you live for Him you can change your life around and gain true inner peace.

Summary

1. Find out why you lack inner peace
2. Looking back at those things and writing them down might help
3. Jesus, the Prince of peace, will heal our emotions and restore our peace if we ask Him

The J Factor:
Joy

"Count it all joy."
The Bible (James 1:2 NKJV)

"To have joy one must share it. Happiness was born a twin."
Lord Byron

Wouldn't you love to be happy no matter what was happening in your life? You can. It's called "Joy". The H Factor isn't about wandering round all the time with an idiotic, false grin on your face even when the dog's died, you've lost your job and your car's blown up! It's more than that. Remember how happiness is defined as the feeling of satisfaction, pleasure or joy? Well, when you don't feel very satisfied because you've been betrayed by a close friend, or you don't feel pleasure because you're in pain, joy can kick in. You can be happy because you have a lasting joy, despite your circumstances.

Joy never leaves you. If you've got it, no one can take it from you. No matter what problems you've got, joy will fill your life. You will find a way to take pleasure in such things as the pattern of sunlight falling through the trees or the sound of the crunch of snow under your feet. If you have joy you can relish these things and it will make your heart sing.

Finding Joy – the Hard Way

Let me tell you how I found it. I'm a pretty confident, positive sort of man. My wife tells me I'm the most optimistic, positive man she knows and perhaps she's right. But in the 1990s I was brought to my knees.

I was the Pastor of a church in Liverpool, England and things were going great, that was until a cult moved nearby. Incredibly, the Pastor of that cult was also called John Partington! He was the same age as I was, the same height as I was, and even had red hair like I had. He had called his church Liverpool Christian Centre and we were called Liverpool Christian Life Centre. The similarities were uncanny.

I found out that this other John Partington had been moving into areas across Britain and calling his cult similar names to churches nearby, posing as a respectable religious group. But they weren't. Instead they were leading people astray. Just after they moved in things went very wrong for me and our church. First of all we were set up by a downmarket Sunday tabloid newspaper who sent their reporter to pose as a distraught husband whose wife had died. He secretly taped the episode and next Sunday the newspaper printed at least eighteen lies in pursuit of a good story. With me in the tabloids, my children started to get verbal abuse at school. Parents in our church started to ask questions about what we really were. All this was in the aftermath of the "Waco" incident in Texas when David Koresh led dozens of people to commit suicide for his warped, cultish aims. We were being tarred with the same brush.

Did I feel happy at this point? No. Everything around me seemed to be crumbling. Depressingly, the problems got worse. One night a predatory homosexual took my fifteen-year-old son out and still wasn't back late at night. I hunted them out and lost my cool with this guy who was much bigger than I was. I was furious and grabbed hold of him. Other things happened to make the circumstances surrounding me seem unbearable. One night a mentally disturbed man attending the church chopped his arm off under a train after hearing me preach a sermon about Jesus metaphorically urging people to cut their arm off if it caused them to sin.

In Despair – but Joy Came

After all this, I came home and got on my knees. I cried out to God that this was it. I couldn't take any more. I wasn't just unhappy, I was completely, totally and utterly finished. Yet, at that moment, a thought came into my mind. It simply said: "It's amazing what praising can do." They are the words of an old Pentecostal chorus that was sung in churches years ago. So I started to praise God, begrudgingly through the pain, the tears, the despair. I was telling God how wonderful He was through gritted teeth. As I was doing this, another thought came: "*Count it all joy.*" That little phrase was from the Bible (James 1:2) where James urged the followers of Christ to thank God for the trials they were going through. I was now doing the same.

> **Something broke in me as I sang praises to God . . .**
> **I was full of joy, despite the pain . . .**
> **No matter what is happening in your life,**
> **shout your praises to God.**

All I can say to you is that something happened in that room I can't explain fully. Something broke in me as I sang praises to God. That might sound strange to you, but that's what happened. I really was counting it all joy. I was full of joy, despite the pain. And that's the secret to joy. No matter what is happening in your life, shout your praises to God. Tell Him how wonderful He is. In the middle of the pain something will break in you too. Remember that happiness will happen in your life if you are feeling this joy. It is a deeper more satisfying form of happiness.

J-O-Y = Jesus, Others, Yourself

It has been said that J-O-Y comes when you put Jesus first, others next and yourself last. And there's truth in that. Focus upon God through your difficulties, trust in Him to bring you through and pray at every opportunity. We're told that as Christians we're going to heaven and that it will be so wonderful we can't even imagine the full wonder of it. Whatever is going on, let God and heaven be your focus. Then look to the interests of others. Ask your work colleagues about what is going on in their lives. Find their passions. Shower your friends with gifts and compliments. Make others happy and you'll be happy too. Finally, consider yourself. You can't be happy by thinking of yourself all the time. All you'll end up doing is feeling worry, fear or anxiety. You'll certainly become a bore! No one wants to be with people who think about themselves all the time. So put yourself last, it really does turn the world on its head, but it's the way to happiness. Jesus said that the whole Bible is summed up by this statement: *"Do to others whatever you would like them to do to you"* (Matthew 7:12 NLT) That's the secret of happiness!

Summary

1. Joy is a deeper expression of happiness
2. Joy can kick in even through pain and difficult circumstances
3. J-O-Y. The secret of getting joy is to put Jesus first, others second, and yourself last
4. Do for others what you would like them to do for you

The K Factor:
Kindness

"Be kind and compassionate to one another."
The Bible (Ephesians 4:32 NIV)

"Love is patient and kind"
The Bible (1 Corinthians 13:4 NLT)

"The little unremembered acts of kindness and love are the
best parts of a person's life."
William Wordsworth

Mother Theresa had it in abundance. So did Lady Diana. Do *you*
have the Kindness Factor? Do you leave your mark on people for
your kindness or do people see you as unkind and ruthless? You
need to become a kinder person if you want to get the H Factor.

Mother Theresa would help the poor amongst the squalor and
chaos in Calcutta. Lady Diana held the hands of Aids' victims and
disadvantaged kids. They had a strong sense of empathy which
resulted in happiness – reaching out to others who are needy.

Easy to Be Unkind

Yet it is all too easy to be unkind. Did you realize that there are
ten times more words in the English language to put people

down than to be kind and build them up? I can call you a fool, stupid or an idiot and hundreds of other names without any problem. But if I want to be kind to you it's not such a simple task! You see, if you believe the newspapers, the world is a dreadfully unkind place. The occasions when we hear of people being kind are hopelessly outnumbered by incidents of road-rage, hate-crime and unkind insults.

> **Did you realize that there are ten times more words in the English language to put people down than to be kind and build them up?**

Many people make a career out of being unkind. Music company executive Simon Cowell has become mega famous in the United States and the UK for being "direct" with those who want to pursue pop stardom. Some people, including Simon, think he is just being honest to the often dreadful singing contestants – but others think he is rude and unkind.

You can still be honest without being unkind. You can still disagree with people without leaving them feeling hurt and put down. The ultimate kindness is to pray for people.

You may get your goals in life. You may be successful and make lots of money. But without having the Kindness Factor you will fail to get the H Factor. Overflowing happiness just isn't possible if you're rude and unkind.

Have a Good Influence on Others

Research indicates that our lives touch the lives of 10,000 other people on average. What sort of effect are you having on those people? Are you being kind to them? God's message to you is full of commands to be kind. In Ephesians 4:32 (NIV) He says to, *"Be kind and compassionate to one another."* In 1 Corinthians 13:4 (NLT) He says that, *"Love is patient and kind."* Get this simple truth. You can't be loving without being kind. You really can't!

In Colossians 3:12 (NIV) the Bible also tells us to, *"clothe yourselves with compassion, kindness, humility, gentleness and patience."* God knows what sort of things you need to get the H Factor. He created us. He knows how important it is for you to "clothed" with this kindness.

People Need Kindness

People really want kindness from you. Even the nastiest hard-guy full of tattoos, hate and venom wants you to be kind to him. Deep down, people crave kindness. Can you give it to them? Think of the unkindest person you know. Adolf Hitler and his war atrocities is an extreme example, but we constantly meet people who are just plain rude. People are not like that because they want to be. They'd love to have the H Factor and to be living life to the full, complete with a life full of kindness.

Incidentally, there is always hope. A good friend of mine, Mark, was one of the most violent criminals in the UK for years and years. He had a broken nose, was a drug addict and dealer, serial thief, burglar and vandal and was tattooed from head to foot with pictures of hate. He wasn't like that because he was happy on the inside. Yet aged thirty he found God through Jesus Christ and now has a heart of love and compassion. In fact, he now leads gangs of troubled youngsters to do gardening and DIY for the elderly! Mark is fast developing the H Factor and leaps out of bed in the morning to embrace the day. Those who are secure and happy want to build others up. Those who are insecure can often come across as rude and unkind.

So where do you rate on the Kindness Factor scale? Think about it right now. Imagine a scale of 0 to 10, 0 representing the kindness level of Adolf Hitler showing virtually no kindness, and 10 relating to Mother Theresa's saint-like devotion to kindness. I must admit that I could be higher up the scale – but we all could. This book – and the H Factor itself – is all about the pursuit of greater things. So, wherever you are on the Kindness Factor scale, never fear! There is always hope.

Kindness Is Powerful

Today, make a conscious decision to reject the unkind part of your character. Write the decision down or underline this part of the book. You need to reject this element and dispel it from your life. Realize that it is never right to be unkind no matter how bad your day has been – never!

> **Today, make a conscious decision to reject the unkind part of your character ... Realize that it is never right to be unkind no matter how bad your day has been – never!**

Remember what Ephesians 4:32 (NIV) says: *"Be kind and compassionate to one another."* Then it adds (NKJV): *"forgiving one another, even as God in Christ forgave you."* If you want to know more about this then read the X Factor later in the book. Because of God's love for you and kindness towards you in His forgiveness for the bad and wrong things in your past, you need to be able to be kind to others.

To get to an even higher stage of kindness, realize that you can do a powerful thing to other people who are down. You can cheer them up with a smile, a positive word or some encouragement. Through your kindness you can reduce someone's stress, you can reduce someone's fear. Or you could be unkind and leave them feeling lousy. It's a choice. How are you relating to the 10,000 or so people you'll effect in a lifetime?

I love this tremendous quote by Mother Theresa, who said, "Let no one ever come to you without leaving better and happier. Be the living expression of God's kindness: kindness in your face, kindness in your eyes, kindness in your smile."

Determine to be different and do it now. When you realize what God did for you by sending His Son to die – the wonderful kindness He has shown to you and me – then you'll want to do kind things for others.

It's Good for Your Health

Freely giving out kindness to all and sundry is good for your health and wellbeing! So why don't you start to blow people away with kindness right now. Resolve that every day you'll do something outrageously kind to someone you barely know. Buy your neighbour some chocolates; leave some cash in the cash machine for the next person to have; pay for the meal of someone you don't know at a restaurant. Watch their reactions. See how great it makes you feel. I did this once in a restaurant in Adelaide, Australia. After my meal I treated another family to their meal by paying the bill. They were shocked but delighted. It was a phenomenal feeling. Try it!

> **Kindness has powerful effects on your health …**
> **Depression can be defeated and**
> **studies show kindness can even**
> **make you live longer!**

Kindness has powerful effects on your health. Research has proved the physical and psychological benefits, often referred to as "helpers high". The endorphins produced can actually block pain. Depression can be defeated and studies show kindness can even make you live longer!

Did you know that a world movement has even been created to recognise and promote kindness? Chuck Wall founded the World Kindness Movement with the realization of the huge benefits brought on by doing kind acts. Chuck realized the benefits of being kind. Have you?

Summary

1. It's all too easy to be unkind
2. We choose whether we touch others' lives with kindness or unkindness
3. Unkind people are unhappy people and are often craving kindness
4. Kindness is powerful
5. Being kind is good for physical and mental health

The L Factor:
Love

CHAPTER 12

> *"For God so loved the world that he gave his one and only Son, that whoever believes in him shall not perish but have eternal life."*
> The Bible (John 3:16 NIV)

> *"Love is patient and kind."*
> The Bible (1 Corinthians 13:4 NLT)

If you don't have love, you've got nothing. And you certainly won't have the H Factor. Love is just about the most overused word in the English language – and perhaps the most misunderstood. Love is well quoted in the vast majority of pop songs that are released. We talk about loving chocolate, our favourite soccer teams, or our work. We even hear talk about "making love".

But real love, real H Factor love, is about sacrifice. It is love that goes the extra mile. It is love that overcomes hate and carries on loving even when others hate you. It is the most potent, powerful and productive force in the world. Do you have love?

Everyone is crying out for love. What do babies need to thrive? Love. What's the ideal motivation for marriage? Love.

Looking at it another way, why do people end up in lives of crime? A lack of love. Why do people kill themselves? A lack of love. The list goes on and on. Why did God sacrifice His Son to save the world? Because He loves it. John 3:16 in the Bible (as you can see from the top of this chapter) tells us so. The Bible is full of love. So what's most important to the God who created you? Love, love, love.

> **Real H Factor love is about sacrifice. It is love that goes the extra mile. It is love that overcomes hate and carries on loving even when others hate you. It is the most potent, powerful and productive force in the world.**

1 Corinthians 13 tells us that if we don't have love then our faith means absolutely zilch. It's nothing. It's dead. Period. Challenging stuff isn't it! I think you get the picture. This thing called love is the most important factor you can have in your life. It is an absolute priority for you to love.

Learning from Big John

I learned that this was the biggest priority in life for every Christian in a powerful way. I was a young pastor at a church in Bedworth in England. One day I got a call to say that "Big John", a new Christian at our church, had been in a serious head-on motorbike accident. The main artery from his heart had been severed and he needed an eight-hour open heart operation. I raced to get to the hospital where he had been taken and saw this 6 foot-plus gentle giant lying on a hospital bed. There were tubes sticking out from his body everywhere. I only had two minutes with him so I squeezed his hand and prayed for him. As

I did so, astonishingly, he opened his eyes. Then he spoke two sentences of three words each that changed my life. He said, "Praise the Lord" and "How are you?"

As I was driving home I couldn't fully comprehend how a man near to death had spoken these words to me. It should have been the other way around. Then it dawned on me that he had his priorities absolutely right. First he said, "Praise the Lord." He was showing that he loved God. Then he said, "How are you?" He was showing that he loved me. I was deeply moved. I then prayed the dumbest prayer anyone can pray. I said, "Dear God, Big John has his priorities right. Will you show me what the greatest priority in life is?" One day God was going to show me. For the record, Big John made a miracle recovery and within one week was sitting up and on his way to being completely well.

Love Is a Priority

In order to share with you how God answered that prayer and what He showed me, first of all, let me tell you what *isn't* to be your priority. It isn't busyness. As a young man I thought that it was. I worked tirelessly in serving God and the church and my young wife Andrene would often be at home. One night a man came to church and said God had told him that my wife at home was hurting. "Don't be silly," I said. That night I told Andrene, whilst nervously laughing, what the man had said and shrugged it off. She began to cry. I learned a hard lesson. He had been right and I was totally ignorant of the facts! Now I advise other men and women that there is no point gaining the whole world if you lose your family in the process. Are you a workaholic? Do you do too much? Are you always busy? Then change before it is too late.

Your priority also isn't popularity, prosperity or possessions.

Let me tell you what it is. Eight years after praying that prayer in the car I woke up on Christmas Day morning to find that one of my eyes had started to protrude out of its socket. I couldn't see out of it. I didn't want to worry Andrene so I kept quiet and instead went to see the doctor. I had weeks of examinations as the eye got worse. They found nothing. I had to have a brain scan and they found a tumour. I needed immediate surgery.

Lack of Love

Just a physical problem you may think, but no. It was because of a spiritual problem too. You see, at the same time as I developed the problem, over a period of time and almost without me knowing it, I was involved in actions not in keeping with a minister of the Gospel. I was also not as loving as I should have been. I had lost my peace, joy and happiness, and my conscience kept me awake at night. I was no longer loving God like the Bible said I needed to. I needed the sin to be removed to help me to see Him clearly again. What was happening physically was mirrored spiritually. I had become spiritually blind.

I had become a professional pastor. I wasn't even reading the Bible as I should. One day I did something that people say you should never do. I opened up the Bible randomly and pointed my finger to see if God would speak. It fell open in the book of Revelation chapter 2 verse 4, which read: "I see what you've done, your hard work, your refusal to quit. I know you can't stomach evil, that you weed out apostolic pretenders. I know your persistence, your courage in my cause, that you never wear out." It was speaking directly to me. Eagerly, I read on. "But you walked away from your first love!" God had spoken in a powerful way to me and I knew it.

Returning to My First Love

I remembered back to my first years of being a Christian aged just fourteen. I loved it. I sang to the Lord Jesus. It was wonderful. I skipped home singing, "How great you are" as I fell in love with Jesus because He was in love with me.

But now I realized that I had lost my first love. I was alone. I prayed, "God, will You help me to find my first love again." It didn't happen straight away and the "surgery" to remove my sin took a long time. The physical surgery on the tumour took a lot less time – and actually was a lot less serious.

I believe most Christians can so easily lose their first love and everyone has to realize that it is really all about loving God. Sadly, most people never actually love the God who made them at all by having a personal relationship with God's Son, Jesus Christ. So if you haven't made a commitment to Jesus, do so today. It's never too late and it doesn't matter how bad you've been in the past.

The Bible tells us that to keep all of God's commandments we have to love God with all our mind, soul and strength and love our neighbour as ourselves (Matthew 22:37–39). So if you love God then you're half way there. Then you need to learn to love those people around you. Those who love God and others have the H Factor.

Do you love your wife like you should do? I have spent more than thirty years determined to do so. Now I'm in love with Andrene far more than when I married her. Love really does grow when you work hard at it. Do you love your friends, neighbours, work colleagues? Do you love your enemies? That's a toughie, but Jesus said that it is easy to love those who love you. He commands that we love those who hate us. Who said being a Christian was an easy life!

If you can love – really love sacrificially – then you can gain the higher levels of happiness. It's a universal law that you reap what you sow. And when you sow love you reap far more love back. Try it!

If you want to know what God looks like, think perfect sacrificial love. "Where love is," said Tolstoy, "God is." Aim for where God is if you want to get the H Factor.

Summary

1. If you don't love, you have nothing
2. Love is the top priority in life
3. Love God first and then those around you as much as you love yourself
4. Sow love and you will have love coming back to you

The M Factor:
Money

"Keep your life free from the love of money,
and be content with what you have."
The Bible (Hebrews 13:5 RSV)

"No servant can serve two masters.
Either he will hate the one
and love the other,
or he will be devoted to the one
and despise the other.
You cannot serve both God and Money."
The Bible (Luke 16:13 NIV)

Money cannot make you happy. Yet desiring more money –
being greedy – is a major cause of unhappiness. Money is
not "the root of all evil", as commonly thought. That mis-
quoted phrase is adapted from the true Bible phrase which
is, *"The love of money is a root of all kinds of evil"* (1 Timothy
6:10 NIV).

There are two common misconceptions which cloud the
whole issue of money:

The Amount Doesn't Matter

It is not the amount of money you have but the way you view it that counts. You could have millions of pounds or dollars yet still want more and more and more. The craving never ends. Your mindset is such that whatever amount you have in the bank will never be enough. It's like sleep – you'll always want five minutes more. I know miserable millionaires. I'm sure that you have read about them. The guy who wins the jackpot on the lottery who sees all his friendships ruined. New people come into his life just for his money. He doesn't know who to trust.

An old woman I heard about was a happy, contented grandmother surviving on a state pension. Then she won a large amount of money in a competition. She died a few years later a bitter and twisted old woman, alienated from her family. Her daughter-in-law suffered mental problems because she didn't receive a big enough slice of the big win. Her son got divorced and her grandson turned to crime and became obese. These are sad, yet all too common results.

If you study the lives of the world's richest men you will see a catalogue of tragedy. Early deaths, loneliness, suicide, divorce, failed friendships, overwork and burnout. It's clear that being financially rich does not spell happiness – in fact, very often it means the opposite.

Comparisons Lead to Misery

In contrast I've seen poverty stricken families in Africa and elsewhere who really have the H Factor! They have a mud-shack for a home, no money, little food and no education. Yet their smiles are big and their happiness levels are high. The reason? They have learned contentment. But they also know little of the "mega bucks" available elsewhere in the world.

People always compare themselves to others. It's a part of human nature. Scientists have conducted research and found that people would prefer to be on a low salary (as long as all their friends and colleagues were on the same salary), than have a higher salary but still earn significantly less than their peers. Bonkers? You bet! But it's human nature. It's the way we operate.

> **Instead of comparing yourself to others, tell yourself you're happy with your lot. And then develop a loose grip on the cash you have. Instead of wanting to see your money grow, develop a giving attitude that will become a habit.**

To get out of this mindset we need to train our brains differently. Our money mindset must change. Start to see money as a means of exchange – as that is simply what it is. It's a means of buying things. Instead of comparing yourself to others, tell yourself you're happy with your lot. And then develop a loose grip on the cash you have. Instead of wanting to see your money grow, develop a giving attitude that will become a habit.

As quickly as I get money in my life I give it away. It's another universal law. The more you give the more you get back. It's true. Try it. The Bible says that you reap what you sow. I've seen this principle pay dividends in my own life. The Bible also says that it is more blessed to give than receive. It means that you are happier when you give than when you get. I also regularly see this truth in my own life. When you give gifts to your small children, nephews or nieces or grandchildren, don't you get a wonderful feeling when you see their beautiful faces light up? That's why giving is better than getting.

Give Your Way to Happiness

Scientific studies also prove another truth. If you give money away to good causes then you will feel happier. The Bible takes it further still. If you give the first part of your income to God through His Church then God will pour out His riches upon you (Malachi 3:10). God is so clear on this that it is the only time in the Bible that He asks us to test Him out on it. He says He will multiply the money back to you many times over. Again, this has happened time and time again in my own life. "Wow!" you may say. And "wow" is the word, perhaps even an understatement! Try it!

> **The world wants you to believe that
> if you get more money then you can buy more for
> yourself and your family and you'll be happier ...
> Rubbish! Don't fall for that lie ... It will raise
> your pleasure level for a few weeks or months
> before the old level of happiness returns.**

The world believes, and wants you to believe, that if you get more money then you can buy more for yourself and your family and you'll be happier. They say a better car, bigger house, new suit, 32-inch plasma TV, etc., etc., will make us happier. Rubbish! Don't fall for that lie. Get out of that mindset. It never will. It will raise your pleasure level for a few weeks or months before the old level of happiness returns ... and the cycle starts all over again. I once read about a study which showed that whether a person won millions on the lottery or became paralysed in an accident, they would return to the same level of happiness they had before the event after six months. Staggering!

Develop a Loose Attachment to Things

Now, don't get me wrong. I'm not knocking all those "nice" things to buy. I have many of them myself, and oh boy, do I enjoy them. At the time of writing this book I have a nice car, Italian suits and a 55-inch telly, yet I have a loose attachment to them. They don't own me. If they went tomorrow I wouldn't bat an eyelid. I'd be as happy if I had a three-wheel van – because my happiness is based on other things in my life.

You need to start to think the same if you want the H Factor. If you want proof that more money does not equal more happiness then just look at the last fifty years in the western world. We've never been richer and have never had so many material goods – yet we're unhappier than we've ever been. There's more crime because people feel envy about other's cars, homes and gadgets. We have more money, but less close friendships, less faith in God and more of a selfish attitude.

In the Bible, Jesus, the Son of God, spoke constantly about money. It shows how important the whole issue is. Jesus said it was harder for a rich man to enter heaven than for a camel to go through the eye of a needle. He meant that people who love money will always put that first before God. Jesus also said that you can't serve God and love money at the same time. Who are you serving?

So start now to get a looser attachment to money. Start to give it away. Give it to your local church – thereby giving it to the God who made you. Give it away to charities. Buy items for people. You will never have happiness if you base your self-worth on your bank account, if you seek more money or if you put money above relationships. As you begin to give your money away your happiness levels will soar.

If you play the lottery every week and feel down when you don't win then you're on dangerous ground. You're placing your hope in something foolish. Even though you're pretty poor you have the "love of money". You may never win and, worse still, if you do win then you're likely to be unhappier than if you hadn't. You'll soon realize that it wasn't the lack of money making you unhappy, but the other things in your life, your attitude, your lack of balance, your lack of fun, good relationships and purpose, as well as the other factors in the H Factor.

Money Can't Make You Happy

But you may be thinking, "What's that Partington on about? Surely we can't be happy if our family is hungry and we don't have enough money to live on?" Well, I believe that there is a "subsistence" level that we need to achieve in order to get the H Factor. This level might be different for different people. We certainly need enough money for good, healthy food, a roof over our heads and clothing. That is a level where – if we have the other Happiness Factors in place – we can still achieve overflowing happiness.

> **You will never have happiness if you base your self-worth on your bank account.**

Now back to what I said at the beginning. Money can't make us happy, but it has the power to destroy our happiness. Most marriages that hit difficult times do so because of money problems. The dreaded "D" word: debt. This is a different matter altogether. Debt can destroy your happiness. It causes worry, stress and anxiety. It pushes thousands to suicide each year. It is a terrible thing. If you're in serious debt then you need professional help – now. Don't delay. The problem won't go away. Seek some professional debt counselling that is reputable and independent. Steer clear of "loan sharks" that want to "consolidate" all your bills into one. They charge crazy levels of interest that will leave you in a far worse state.

A recent opinion poll by Gfk NOP revealed that people in Britain are far less happy today then they were in the 1950s – despite being three times richer! There are similar figures in America and Australia ... in fact across the western world. Incidentally, the same study showed that 48 percent of respondents believed relationships and not money is the key to happiness.

Earn More Than You Spend

If you have credit cards my general advice is to chop them up, unless you pay them off every month. Start to save some money for a rainy day. Make a budget listing all your incomings and outgoings each month. Alter any spending to ensure you're earning more than you spend and cut out unnecessary expenditure such as a second car and social spending such as tobacco, alcohol and takeaway food. Once you're starting to earn more than you spend, you're on the right course. Buy *The Money Secret* by Rob Parsons for more excellent advice on these issues.

Summary

1. Remember, money can't make you happy, but debt has the power to destroy your happiness
2. Give your way to happiness
3. Get financial advice if you're in bad debt
4. Give to God through His local church ... and watch the windows of blessing open!
5. Develop a loose attachment to money

The N Factor:
Negativity

Negativity has the power to destroy your happiness. It can extinguish your energy. It's that powerful. It's destructive, dangerous and devastatingly life destroying. I've watched so many people fail to find true happiness because they have developed this negativity habit. It's tragic.

If love and generosity are the top two causes of the H Factor, then sin followed by negativity are two of the top robbers of it! A negative person will never understand the place of contentment.

Have you ever heard of the Greek god "Dis"? Well stick that word on the front of some positive words and you'll get some pretty unpleasant ones. Put it on to courage and you'll get discourage; put it on to empower and you'll get disempower; put it before content and you'll get discontent. It has been said that people live in one of two tents: content or discontent! Happy people are contented people.

Thoughts Are Powerful

Some people never enjoy the journey of life because their daily life is taken over by horrible, unhelpful thoughts that do them no good. They spend their time thinking negatively about everything. You can't enjoy the journey that way. Rid yourself of all sick thoughts – hate, resentment, inferiority, and the like. These kind of thoughts can very often lead to depression. Thoughts are vital. You choose what they are, either negative or positive. You're thinking right now. You'll be thinking when you wash your hands, watch the television and make the tea. Negativity is linked to your attitude – your mindset. So many people need to get a different mindset. We need to put on the spectacles of optimism and to go out of our way to speak optimistically about everything. Do you?

Bars or Stars?

Two men are in prison. One sees bars, the other sees stars. Which are you? Think of your mind like a train track. A train is constantly driving round your brain and whatever it carries when it hits the front of the head is the thought you carry. Now imagine that you are the train operator. You are in charge. You decide what thoughts are put onto the train. The more positive thoughts you think, the more positive your entire thought process becomes. If you think negative thoughts and put them on the train, they will make you a negative person.

This means that you can change the flow of negativity. You can conquer it. You can become a new you, all by defeating your negative thoughts. However, it may take some time. I would say it is virtually impossible to have overflowing happiness if you are – to put it bluntly – a moaning old so and so. I must admit I don't even like being around negative people and I choose my friends accordingly!

A lady I know called Kirsty once repelled everyone because of her negative attitude. She carried a cloud with her wherever she went. People would pretend they weren't home when she popped round for coffee and she couldn't understand why she didn't have any friends. Now, however, she has realized her deep negativity and is making an effort to change her mind to have good, positive thoughts. Do you recognise yourself in that description? Are people avoiding you? Change your thoughts. Start to speak positively. The Bible says to "*. . . let God transform you into a new person by changing the way you think*" (Romans 12:2 NLT). Meditate on that scripture.

Dealing with Hurts

Very often people are negative because they are negative about themselves, because they are hurting people. People who don't think very highly of themselves, who are insecure, will often pull other people down. You can change by dealing with your inner self. Prayer to God for inner healing is crucial. Just ask Him daily to start doing a healing of your childhood hurts, bitterness, rejection, and all the negative thoughts you received in the home. There are many good books on this process. This healing could take a little time but is vital.

Become a Positive Person

Another group of people are negative because they've got into the negativity habit. This is easily done. We're in a world that mostly takes the negative viewpoint. Watch the news, read the newspapers or look at a television soap opera. It's negative, negative, negative! It takes some force to swim against this tsunami of negativity. If you're in this group of people then you need to start to swamp your mind with positive thoughts. Write down the words "Be Positive" and pin them up around your home and at your workplace. Every time you start to be negative imagine a huge sign saying "STOP" being put up in your mind. Then replace the negative thought with a positive one. Do this consistently and over several days – usually between three and six weeks – your mind's thoughts will start to change. It really works!

> **Write down the words "Be Positive" and pin them up around your home and at your workplace. Every time you start to be negative imagine a huge sign saying "STOP" being put up in your mind.**

Guard Your Life from Negative People

Perhaps you're in a third group of people. This group are negative because all their friends are negative. As much as you can, you need to get these negative people out of your life. It's true that like attracts like. Birds of a feather flock together. And if you're trying to break free from a spirit of negativity then you need to be around positive people. Who are your friends?

Reflect on yourself now. On a scale of 1 to 10, where 1 represents you being very negative and 10 very positive, where would you be? If you're less than 5 then you will likely need some urgent and determined work to turn your thoughts around. You will need to be brutal with yourself and recognise there is a problem before you can deal with it.

Think of the downside of your being negative. You put people off wanting to be with you. You bring your own mood down. You put the moods of others down. Why on earth would you want to be like that!? Those with the H Factor are positive all the time. They reflect on negative situations with positive thoughts. So practice positive thoughts until you become excited – and exciting!

The Power of Positive Thinking

One writer who has popularised this teaching in recent years is the late Norman Vincent Peale, writer of the "Power of Positive Thinking" books. Peale believed that thoughts were critically important. And he was right. He also contended that we need the power of belief to carry our positive thoughts through. Again, he was absolutely spot on. You see, you need to think thoughts that are vital for the happy life. You have to stop thinking bad thoughts about other people. You need to banish destructive thoughts from your mind – thoughts of anger, jealously, plotting, selfishness and hate. You also need to believe that you can be happy. You need to believe that you can have the H Factor.

I believe that I can do anything. When I go into a challenge I take good, positive thoughts with me. I try to think good thoughts about everyone I meet. I try to speak positively about others. I keep negative people away from my close circle of friends. Their influence is like a bad stench in a room. It spreads. Get them out of your life or at least help them to change!

When most people think they are being "realistic" they delude themselves. They are simply being negative. Your thoughts will play a massive role in helping you to get the H Factor. The Bible tells us in Proverbs 23:7 (NKJV) that *"As* [a man] *thinks in his heart, so is he."* In other words, you become what you believe. The way you think is the direction you are heading in! Kick the negativity habit today.

Summary

1. Negativity will rob you of the H Factor
2. Get rid of negative thoughts by changing your mindset and developing new habits
3. Deep hurts can be healed
4. Having negative people around you does not help
5. Practise the positive principle – the principle that "all things are possible"

The O Factor: *Obstacles* (and how to overcome them!)

"Do just once what others say you can't do,
and you will never pay attention to
their limitations again."
James R. Cook

"Stand up to your obstacles and do something about them.
You will find that they haven't half the strength
you think they have."
Norman Vincent Peale

*"In this world you will have trouble.
But take heart! I have overcome the world."*
Jesus (John 16:33 NIV)

There are loads of obstacles to the H Factor. You need to know what they are and how to overcome them. These include low self-esteem, worry, negativity, fear and discontentment. Remember that our original definition of happiness shows that you are happy when you feel satisfaction, joy or pleasure. We must be aware then of the things that can stop you feeling satisfaction and pleasure and that can threaten your joy.

Defeat Fear

One of the most popular of these robbers is fear. It's a short word but it has great power. Fear can stop you living your dream. Fear can leave you feeling miserable every day. Fear can even make you sick. In short, fear will put out the light of your happiness. Fear is to being happy what water is to fire. It is a modern-day disease. Everyone seems to be affected by it. To get out of it people turn to alcohol or drugs, or they opt out from real living.

> **You can't learn how to be ecstatically happy without knowing the obstacles to happiness – and how to overcome them.**

No matter what your dream is, how much money you've got, how much fun you have, how balanced you are, what your integrity is like – you can't be happy and live in fear. It can't happen. Fear is a robber. It prevents you from sleeping, causes illnesses and can even be "caught" by those around you.

So what's the best way to defeat fear? Admit it, find the cause and face it. You may have heard the phrase "feel the fear and do it anyway". That's absolutely right! Whenever a nagging fear creeps up on you, acknowledge it and do the thing you fear regardless.

As you know, I'm a Christian minister and I can tell you with absolute assurance that seeking God is the best cure for fear. The Bible contains the phrase "do not fear" 365 times, which means there is one for every day of the year! Obviously God knows what a crippling and destructive thing it can be. And what is fear the opposite of? Faith! The more faith you have that Almighty God is with you and fighting for you, the less of a hold fear will have on your life. I said that fear is a great power, but even greater than that is faith. The more faith you have, the less fear will hamper your happiness. Ask God for help to rid you of fear. Then believe – really believe – that God is helping you. I know of one young man called Dave whose parents divorced when he was eleven. After that devastating event he had a mini-breakdown and fear got hold of his life, so much so that he contemplated suicide in his late teens. But in his early twenties he discovered the God of the Bible in a real relationship. Now he has learned to overcome any fear by a strong confidence in God and I'd say he has the makings of the H Factor. You can have it too. Defeat fear today.

Win Over Worry

Another robber of happiness is a cousin of fear and is equally destructive. It's called worry. This seems to be another modern-day disease. We spend half our time worrying about things that never, ever happen. Then we feel burnt out because we've used up valuable energy we needed to deal with everyday life. Pointless!

> **Jesus tells us to focus on the day at hand and don't even think of tomorrow. What brilliant advice! And it's a great way to win over worry. Try it.**

Let's look at the letters in the word "Worries". W-O-R-R-I-E-S can W-ear you down, O-bstruct your creativity, R-ob you of joy and sleep, R-uin your life, I-gnite stress, E-nd your hope and S-end you to an early grave! It can bring about ulcers, migraines, bowel problems and much more. Yes, worry can kill you. You need to get rid of it.

The things we worry about include money, death, health,

loneliness, unemployment and the end of the world. The list goes on and on! Again, we can look to the Bible for the solution. In the book of Matthew, Jesus tells us to focus on the day at hand and don't even think of tomorrow. What brilliant advice! And it's a great way to win over worry. Try it.

Another way to rid your life of worry is to get things into perspective. Is that tea stain on your jeans or that rude person in the shop really that important? If you place your worry against some major things in the world – famine, pain, disasters – they mean very little indeed.

Rocky Ride

Recently, on a plane trip to South Africa I was sat next to a huge – I mean really huge – lady. On top of that, the man in front of me pushed his seat right back. So for the whole ten hours I was incredibly uncomfortable. I had to change my attitude and tell myself to take control by realizing there was nothing I could do. I had a choice: I could be irritated, angry and bogged down by this, or I could enjoy the journey despite the circumstances. I told myself that it could be worse, it could have been a twenty-four-hour flight!

You can also help to defeat worry by focusing on others. When you start to look to the needs of others, worrying about your own problems can fade. In addition, you could take yourself a whole lot less seriously. Laugh at your problems! How many times a day do you laugh? Remember that the average child laughs about 150 times a day and the average adult only four to eight times a day. Lighten up a bit. Re-read the F Factor chapter! Finally, as is the case when dealing with fear, you can increase your faith in God to help banish worry. The more you read the Bible and pray, the more your worry will evaporate.

Raise Your Self-esteem

The third robber of happiness in your life is low self-esteem. This can have several causes. If it is caused by a difficult childhood then you need to identify where that started. You may need to identify when you started to feel bad about yourself and to replace your negative thoughts about yourself with positive ones. So if you have been told that you're stupid and will never amount to anything, tell yourself that you have worth and are capable of achieving your dreams. Your sub-conscious mind will believe anything it is told. You could have been told lies about yourself as a child. Now is the time to start to change that. Low self-esteem will stop you having the happiness level you deserve. I don't know anyone with low self-esteem who has the H Factor. It may take a while to start to believe you're of worth but it is possible.

There is nothing more effective than asking the God who made you and loves you to heal your low self-esteem. Meditate on the fact that the God who made you wants the best for you. He sees you as you really are – beautiful and brilliant. Your low self-esteem might have been caused by thoughts that you are ugly, overweight, stupid, from the wrong family. It's all wrong! It's all lies. You are who you are because God made you and loves you. The Bible tells us that you were perfectly made. You were! You are! Really take these truths in. Reflect on them before you go to bed at night and write them on some paper and attach it to your bathroom mirror. Tell yourself that in God's eyes you are brilliant, beautiful, clever, capable and worth so much – because it's true.

Low self-esteem can be the cause of low confidence and this is a major problem in you having the H Factor. Start to chal-lenge these bad assumptions believed by your subconscious. Replace those self-defeating thoughts with thoughts of "I can".

One of the best statements made in the Bible is: *"I can do all things through Christ who strengthens me."* Let this be the mantra of your life. Don't let anything rob you of the H Factor.

Summary

1. Low self-esteem, worry, negativity, fear and discontentment are all robbers of the H Factor. Learn how to overcome them

2. To overcome fear: admit it, find the cause and face it. Face what you fear and do it anyway!

3. To overcome worry: take Jesus' advice and focus on today. Get things into their true perspective

4. To raise your self-esteem: ask God to heal your low self-esteem. Remind yourself constantly that in God's eyes you are brilliant and beautiful

The P Factor:
Purpose

"The only true happiness comes from
squandering ourselves for a purpose."
William Cowper (1731–1800)

*"Many are the plans in a man's heart,
but it is the Lord's purpose that prevails."*
The Bible (Proverbs 19:21 NIV)

Do you want to wake up eager with excitement to start the day? Then find your purpose.

Do you know what you've been born for? Do you know your calling, your destiny, your purpose?

I sincerely hope you do because you can't be fully happy without it. Without it you will never find true happiness.

Elvis Presley was known as the King of Rock and Roll and is still hugely popular today. Yet, despite his talent he died aged only forty-two after falling into over-work, obesity, drug abuse and depression. Elvis lacked a proper purpose even though he eventually committed his life to Jesus Christ.

Other people the world over go to the grave never realizing why they were put on earth. Perhaps they have had a successful marriage and career, but have fallen short of a great purpose and therefore overflowing happiness. Perhaps this is you?

If you're reading this thinking you really don't know what your purpose it, don't fret. You can find it. That's a promise. That's what this chapter is about.

I often wonder what's most important, the push of the past or the pull of the future. You see, you have a past and you can't alter it or deny it. It's made you what you are today. But your future, hopes, aspirations and purpose for being provides the most powerful basis for your happiness.

Live Long and Be Happy

You need to seek a purpose for your life with all your being. A purpose will help you to get up in the morning. A purpose will carry you through each day. It will keep you living long beyond a normal life span. So often you see people retire from their jobs and settle back into slow, easy living. Then they die. You can't live if there is nothing to live for. And even if you are physically alive you'll just be going through the motions . . . existing more than living.

Former British Prime Minister Margaret Thatcher, "The Iron Lady", was driven in her purpose to rid the world of socialism. She trained herself to have only four hours sleep each night so she could pursue her passion and purpose. She would say: "If socialists get up at 5.00am then I'll get up at 4.00am." That's a passion. That's purpose. Sadly, however, Mrs Thatcher wouldn't get the H Factor as she also struggled to relax or take time out for real fun. Many of her friends claim she was driven to live for her cause.

Recent research by scientists in Sweden revealed just how important finding your purpose is to being happy. Research leader Dr Bengt Bruelde claimed money, love and success only bring temporary joy. Instead, he said, working hard to achieve a goal is the key. He added, "Striving to achieve something by work gives a purpose to life and this is the meaning of true happiness. Sitting in the sun with nothing to do is not a sure-fire recipe for a contented life."

Dr Bruelde is so convinced that working towards a purpose is the key that he says many holidaymakers are happier working for their break than they are lying on a hot beach. He said, "People are happiest when they face and conquer a challenge which is outside their normal routine." So set yourself a goal that you've just got to reach. Then build under it a fire of anticipation and keep it burning. That goal will keep beckoning. And when you reach your goal, still new goals will succeed it. These are the self-perpetuating motivators of enthusiasm.

Passionate About Purpose

So what could your purpose be? Evil Adolf Hitler had a purpose to see Germany take over the world with his perverse "super-race" ideas. Some people unashamedly want to make as much money as anyone else in the world – just so they can say they're filthy rich. Others live their purpose out by looking after their family. Some have a moral purpose to set up a children's home, to feed the poor or cancel out poverty. Former pop star Bob Geldof has been driven by his desire to tackle world poverty. He has been the man to organise huge pop concerts across the world. That's a passion for a purpose. The Bible says that God has a plan and a purpose for your life, a plan to do you good and not to do you harm, a plan to give you hope and a future (Jeremiah 29:11). What's yours?

The Purpose Driven Life

The most powerful teaching I've heard on purpose is from the Californian pastor Rick Warren of Saddleback Church. He wrote the book, *The Purpose Driven Life*,[4] which has sold more than 30 million copies. It's proven so popular because everyone wants to find their purpose. Everyone wants to know why they've been born and what they've been born for.

Rick sums up everyone's life as having five primary purposes. He believes we're all made to love God, to serve God and others, to be friends with other Christians, to grow to be like Jesus, and to share our good news about God's love with others. He believes that we're all made to fulfil these five purposes and that people who do these things have a life in balance. I'd agree with him, in fact I'm passionate about this teaching.

> **To be frank, you get happy by living for others ...**
> **Seek to serve others instead of living for yourself**
> **and you'll get happy.**

Rick is right in his assertion that everyone worships *something*, whether it's a pop star like Madonna, a football team such as Liverpool F.C., or plain old money. That's worship. But the best thing to worship is the God who made you. Worship involves the way you live each day. It affects your lifestyle. If you worship God then you should live each day for God. That means you don't lie, cheat or steal as part of your worship to God. Instead you live the type of life you know the Bible talks about. If you put God first in your life the Bible says that God will direct your paths. Isn't that a brilliant promise!

We were all made to serve God and we serve God by serving others. To be frank, you get happy by living for others. The old song said, "Make someone happy and you'll be happy too." And it's true! Seek to serve others instead of living for yourself

[4] Rick Warren, *The Purpose Driven Life*, Zondervan Publishing House, 2003.

and you'll get happy. I'm a natural evangelist. I get no better feeling than when I am sharing my faith in God with someone else.

If you haven't already done so, I'd wholeheartedly recommend you getting a copy of *The Purpose Driven Life*. These principles are changing lives all across the world. They work!

Spiritual Living

We don't live in a world without a spiritual dimension. We live in a natural/spiritual universe that contains things we can see and things we can't. As we live out God's purpose for our lives, we need to develop the spiritual side of our life. You can't find a better purpose in life than to live for Almighty God.

God came to earth 2,000 years ago as Jesus Christ. Jesus' purpose was to "seek and save" those who are lost (Luke 19:10). The Church today has the same purpose – to reach the lost for Jesus Christ. What God means by "the lost" is those who don't yet know Jesus as the only way to God and who don't live for Him; those who don't know or who haven't accepted God's love and grace.

Jesus gave His life on the cross for His purpose. What's yours?

Summary

1. You can find your purpose in life
2. Pursuing your purpose will help you to live long and be happy
3. Read Rick Warren's book *The Purpose Driven Life*
4. Jesus gave His life for His purpose – to reach you and me

The Q Factor:
Quality

"Remember that happiness is a way of travel –
not a destination."
Roy M. Goodman

"Finally, brothers, whatever is true,
whatever is noble, whatever is right,
whatever is pure, whatever is lovely,
whatever is admirable – if anything is excellent
or praiseworthy – think about such things."
The Bible (Philippians 4:8 NIV)

You are top quality. You were perfectly made. Even if you reckon you're fat, thick, have the wrong coloured hair or a big nose, you've still been created with excellence. God doesn't make mistakes. And that's exactly the way we need to think about everything we do in life. It has to be done with excellence. A creative little boy on a farm once sent his arrow hurtling out of his bow to hit the garden shed. He then whipped out a tin of paint and drew a target around his arrow. He'd got his bull's eye! The point is clear. We must aim at something or else we'll hit nothing.

Don't Settle for Second Best

We need to do our very best in everything. We were made with a purpose in mind. So many people fail to achieve their potential because they fail to seek excellence. Being second best or mediocre is not an option for those seeking the H Factor.

For example, how we dress speaks volumes about us. When we look good we feel good! Have you ever had that great feeling you get when you put on a new, crisply ironed shirt? Wow, doesn't it make you feel good! That's a glimpse of quality.

> **Are you putting your all into what you do?
> And do you look for quality in your relationships,
> your friends, your children, your marriage?
> Why settle for second best in anything?**

How are you in your work life? Are you putting your all into what you do? And do you look for quality in your relationships, your friends, your children, your marriage? Why settle for second best in anything? I always aim to win. If I'm playing snooker, chess, doing public speaking or hosting a party at my home I aim for the best. You deserve it. Others deserve it. God deserves it. When you give your best you say something about yourself, about other people, and the God you serve.

Think Quality Thoughts

Are you aiming at quality? Do you realize just how much potential quality you have within you? Let me tell you that you have bags of potential! Whether you utilise your potential all depends on the quality of your thoughts. Are you telling yourself that you can do something well, that you have the potential of real quality? Or do you attempt things believing deep down that you're really not that good? Constantly re-emphasise to yourself that God has built potential quality into your nature. By affirming it and practising it, it will grow and strengthen within you just as muscles do.

A flea was kept in a jam jar and tried desperately to jump out but repeatedly hit his head on the lid. When the lid was lifted off do you think he could jump out of the jam jar? Well he could have, if he had realized the potential and the quality that he had within him. But the lid had kept him down for so long that he failed to rise any higher than the jam jar lid. He had been conditioned to believe that he couldn't rise any higher. His thinking kept a lid on his potential. Quality says "yes" to rising up and achieving your best and "no" to accepting mediocrity. It's the least you deserve.

Go for Excellence

Regardless of what line of work you happen to be in, you always need to aim for quality. The churches I have led have all strived for excellence. There is a standard of excellence in the décor, the way the services are run, even the coffee afterwards! The same principles must apply to your profession, be it education, the police, cleaning, whatever. Sloppy behaviour is a sign that you're not totally happy with yourself.

Let's aim for excellence in our relationships – with God, our spouses and our family and friends. Let's go for quality in the way we show hospitality. Edge Church International where I'm a pastor has a culture of going for top-notch hospitality which is so important. So the welcome for visitors is very friendly and the standard of care and follow-up of people is excellent. During conferences our food is of the standard of any top restaurant.

If I have friends over I'll go the extra mile in making them feel welcome. That's excellence. I'll make sure my car, suit and shoes are clean. That's quality. If I have a meeting booked in, I'll turn up – and on time! That's quality. The list goes on and on.

> **Regardless of what line of work you happen to be in, you always need to aim for quality ...**
> **Sloppy behaviour is a sign that you're not totally happy with yourself.**

Changing your approach to one of constantly raising your standards will inevitably be noticed by others. You might even get criticised or discouraged because of it, but don't be put off. Just do the very best you can and then put an imaginary umbrella up over your head to keep that rain of criticism from touching you.

Don't let any hindrance stop you. Always remember that you have spiritual and mental qualities within you that can overcome even the seemingly impossible. Right now you need to answer this important question: what quality of life do you want? Then you need to go for it. When you expect the best, you release a magnetic force in your mind, which has the tendency to attract the best to you! Let quality become the guiding stick for your life. Aim at nothing less.

Some say that if I fell into a cow pat I'd come up smelling of roses! This isn't true but there is something in it. I always expect the best and an excellent belief pattern gets excellent results!

Summary

1. You are top quality – you were made that way
2. To achieve your full potential in life, you have to put in your best quality effort and not be satisfied with second best
3. Don't hold yourself down by accepting mediocrity. Expand your thinking and go for releasing the quality that is within you
4. If you want to have quality of life then you have to strive for excellence in everything you do

CHAPTER

18

The R Factor:
Relationships

"Let us be grateful to people who make us happy. They are
the charming gardeners who make our souls blossom."
Marcel Proust

"Greater love has no one than this,
that he lay down his life for his friends."
Jesus (John 15:13 NIV)

Do you have close friends? If you don't then you need to find
some if happiness is your goal.

Relationships are critical to your happiness. If you're lonely
because of a lack of friends and family or you have weak
relationships then you'll never find real happiness. That's a
powerful truth and you need to believe it. Relationships are that
important.

University studies confirm that relationships are a crucial
factor in the eternal search for a happy, fulfilled life. Try and
think of one truly happy person who doesn't have good
relationships with other people. I bet you can't. Yet people
who have a network of great friendships and family relationships are the happiest of all. I said in an earlier chapter that if
you have one great friend in a lifetime then you're very rich – in

which case I feel like a millionaire! I'm loaded with them. I spend time nurturing friendships and relationships. They are vital to me. Relationships are more vital than power, position, prestige . . . or anything else for that matter.

> **Relationships are critical to your happiness. If you're lonely because of a lack of friends and family or you have weak relationships then you'll never find real happiness . . . Relationships are that important.**

In contrast loneliness is a killer of happiness and a modern day disease. Countless millions of people know the agony of having no good friends. What a terrible tragedy.

Relationships Are Vital

In 2004 I discovered that one of my great friends and a mentor in the Christian faith, Frank Houston, had died. I left what I was doing in Exeter, England, drove four hours to London then travelled for thirty hours to Australia just to attend the funeral. The relationship I had with Frank meant that much to me.

Very often people become bitter in life because of a failed relationship such as a broken marriage, friendship or fall out with a brother or sister. But we all need to recognise that relationships are vital to our happiness. It's the same with family relationships. With these I've had to learn the hard way. In my children's early years I put my work in Christian ministry above that of my wife and family. Wrong, wrong, wrong. I had become out of balance. I had lost sight of the God-given priorities I should have been basing my life on. For me, my relationship with God always comes first. Then it's my relationship with my wife, then my children, then my work and ministry at the church. That's the right order. We were made for relationship. It is the key to success in our career, our family and our social life. Even if our work or business or church life doesn't go how we want, it is less important than relationships with our family and friends.

Build Great Relationships

If you want to get happier, to strive towards the H Factor, then you need to build strong and lasting relationships. Some of my closest and best friendships were built at school, youth group and church some forty years ago! That doesn't mean I'm exclusive, I always look to increase my number of relationships daily! Don't imagine that relationships are easy to build however. They are costly, painful and time consuming – but totally essential for true happiness.

Relationships, for me, are what my faith in God, my Christianity, is all about. The essence of Christianity is a relationship with Almighty God, made possible because He came down to earth 2,000 or so years ago as a human being, Jesus Christ. More of this in the X Factor chapter. You know what, and you may be shocked at this. I hate religion. I mean it. I can't stand anything that is religious. That's because I don't follow a religion. Religion is about following rules, traditions and customs and doing things a certain way. That is not Christianity. My faith is about a relationship with God. It is about talking to God in prayer through Jesus Christ in a personal manner and then listening as God speaks back to you. God is into relationships big time. I worship Him as the God that guides my life, because He has a personal, individually tailored plan for my life.

Your Spouse and Family Are Important

Second only to my relationship with God is the relationship I
have with my wife and family. I look to develop my relationships with them by spending time together. Actually, my wife
and kids are my very best friends. Beyond my family I look to
my friends and I try to enrich their lives and in turn this enriches
my life. Wherever I go, be it the butchers, bakers or bagel
makers, I look to build relationships. I'm never happier than
when making friends, having a good laugh and looking to make
the world a bit of a better place by nurturing relationships. I
believe that this social dimension of life enhanced through
relationship building is a vital contributory factor to overflowing happiness.

If someone makes a mistake and does something that is
potentially damaging to their relationship with me, I don't look
to condemn them or "point the finger". You have to remember
that we are all human, and all capable of doing things we later
regret. I know of so many incidents in ministry where someone
has fallen morally and others have simply given up on them.
That's a devastating blow to the person when they're probably
already feeling lousy. If you've ever succumbed to pointing the
finger at someone else, let me advise you to rethink your
actions now. It could be you falling next time! Instead of
criticising and judging we have to see how we can carry on
building and nurturing those relationships. And never put
people on pedestals – they can only be knocked down. Try to
find out the factors in someone's life that has made them hit
hard times. Seek to understand and to wear someone else's
shoes. Be a relationship developer. Look for the opportunities
wherever you go.

This need for relationships has been built into us by God. It is
a real need. That's why, as we're told in the Bible, God made

Eve in the Garden of Eden, as company for Adam. *"It is not good for man to be alone,"* God said (Genesis 2:18). We were made for relationship. Think of those people who don't have good relationships and you'll have an unhappy person. They'll be lonely. They will fail to reach high levels of happiness. They'll have no one to share their success with. They'll have no one to encourage them when they're down.

> **Find people who are lonely and love them unconditionally.**

If you're a Christian and want to pursue God's heart then reach those who aren't yet Christians with practical love. Develop relationships and show the love of Jesus to them. Pray for them. Prayer changes things in a powerful way. Find people who are lonely and love them unconditionally. God's heart is to reach everyone who doesn't yet live for Him in order to build His family. If you do this you'll be sharing in the passion and purpose of Almighty God – an extra bonus in finding happiness.

Start right now to develop your relationships. Invest a lot in those relationships that are most important to you. For instance, put this book down and take your wife out! Phone your son and ask how his life is going. Meet your mate for coffee. Ask the next door neighbour what his plans are for the coming year. Buy your work colleague lunch and find out their life dream. Reach the hurting, the desperate, the lonely. Build those relationships now!

Summary

1. Relationships are critical to your happiness
2. Invest time into developing your relationships – especially those which are the most important.
3. Put your relationship with God first, your partner (if you have one) second, other family members next and then your friends
4. Have compassion when someone makes a mistake and threatens to ruin your relationship with them
5. Look for opportunities to develop new relationships

The S Factor: *Sacrifice*

"In this world it is not what we take up,
but what we give up, that makes us rich."
Henry Ward Beecher

"The greatest among you will be your servant."
Jesus (Matthew 23:11 NIV)

Here we have a crucial key to happiness – sacrifice. Or in other words, living for others instead of just yourself. Those who have the H Factor live to make others happy. They often forget themselves and think about how their wife, a friend, a colleague or even strangers can best be pleased. It sounds ridiculous but it is a universal truth. There's an old song which has a line in it which sums it up: "Make someone happy and you'll be happy too." Wonderful! I've put this into practice and know that it works. You must grasp this truth. Remember how wonderful you felt when you did a good turn to someone else. You possibly felt a "rosy glow" inside. That was you being happy; truly, deeply happy.

The world is full of people who are miserable and in desperate need. Look upon your work as serving others and it will transform your whole life. What can you do in your spare time to help someone's loneliness? Could you help the poor, the oppressed, the hungry? Perhaps you could join a charity, visit a lonely old person or write to someone in prison? Whatever it is, lose your life in this way and you will surely find it.

The "Me" Culture

Too often we go through life seeking only to gain what we want, what we think will make us happy, what the world tells us is good for us. We seek bigger houses, bigger pay cheques, bigger cars. As we saw in an earlier chapter, statistics show us that the rise in materialism in the western world has actually made us far less happy. Living for ourselves just doesn't work. The term "oneism" has been invented by some to sum up this modern day curse of extreme selfishness. It's the "me" culture that prevails. People are seeking divorces because they know that they will get big payoffs – and they fight to get the best result for them out of it! Yet, if a married couple died to themselves and lived for each other an amazing marriage would result.

> **If we live for others and forget self,**
> **it's a fast track to happiness.**

It's true that we're all made selfish. We're out for our own interests by our very human nature. However, that is the easy way to live. You don't have to learn that way of living. Children live that way, naturally. They don't have to be taught to be selfish. Ask any parent! Yet, it's also true that if we continue to live this way then we'll end up unhappy at some point. There's nothing so sure, and as I've already said, the reverse is also true. If we live for others and forget self, it's a fast track to happiness.

This is what sacrifice is all about. Think of those people you know who are deliriously happy. Aren't they people who seem to care for others? Find some arrogant, selfish and rude person and you'll no doubt have someone numbingly unhappy on the inside.

Find a Cause Worth Fighting

Think of some people you know you who sacrifice their lives for good causes or ideals. Aren't they happy? Though so many soldiers perished in the last world wars they were sacrificing their lives to win freedom against evil forces that threatened to take over the world. That was the cause that spurred many of them on. You can maybe think of someone local to you who fought for a particular cause for years. They sacrifice time and energy to fight for safer roads, a cure for cancer or a better world. By throwing themselves into a passion for something that others will benefit from they make themselves happy. Living a life sitting alone on a hot beach sipping cool Coke might sound like a dream come true. But it can never result in true, real happiness. It's more likely to bring about emptiness.

Sacrifice in the Little Things

Practically speaking, you don't need to fight in a war, die for the neighbour's dog or give up your home for a vagrant in order to get happy. You can simply live your life one day at a time looking out for others before yourself. If you are married then set out to make sure your husband or wife is the happiest person alive. Buy them a present, bring them breakfast in bed, find out their dream and help them to achieve it. As happiness grows in their life, watch it soar in yours too – and watch your marriage sizzle!

Forget trying to please yourself by living for yourself. It can't be done. Instead, live for others. The more you think of others the happier you will be.

Perhaps you could just live for those around you? Look to pick someone up regularly for work, even though it is out of your way. Ask someone about their problems and forget about your own. Write to a pen pal in a third world country, sponsor a child or buy a mountain goat for a remote African village. Take a mate out for the birthday of a lifetime or clean the litter from your road. Whatever it is, do it. Get out of yourself. Stop moaning about irrelevant, petty problems and focus on some-one else who has a mountain to climb. Forget trying to please yourself by living for yourself. It can't be done. Instead, live for others. The more you think of others the happier you will be.

Summary

1. Living a selfish and materialistic life only leads to unhappiness
2. People who give up their time for good causes are usually happy
3. Living life doing small things to make others happy will make you happy too
4. The more you think of others the happier you will be

The T Factor:
Thankfulness

"A thankful heart is not only the greatest virtue,
but the parent of all other virtues."
Cicero

"Feeling gratitude and not expressing it
is like wrapping a present and not giving it."
William Arthur Ward

*"We give thanks to God always for you all,
making mention of you in our prayers."*
The Bible (1 Thessalonians 1:2 NKJV)

It's a wonderful thing to be thankful throughout this short life. The happiest people in the world are usually those who are the most thankful. If you're thankful then you're probably very content. Contentment is the sister of thankfulness.

Contentment Leads to Happiness

Discontentment is a destroyer of happiness. That's when you look for every reason to moan about your lot in life. It's when you refuse to look at the wonderful things that are happening and focus instead of what you haven't got and how you're worse off than your friends, the people on the television adverts, even the people who lived 200 years ago!

Discontentment – a lack of thanks for all sorts of things in your life – will block your quest for happiness. Guaranteed. The British rock band the Rolling Stones famously sang the song "I can't get no satisfaction" in the seventies. Isn't that still true of this modern age? No wonder happiness appears such a rare thing and yet everyone is seeking it ... very often unsuccessfully.

True Happiness Escapes Most People

What most people don't realize is that no matter how much money they have, no matter how good looking their partner is, no matter how fit their body is, they can never be happy if they're not content in the first place. It's impossible. They spend a fortune looking for all sorts of things, yet true happiness still escapes them.

So to get happy you need to start getting into the habit of giving thanks. Be thankful for everything you've got in life. That's one thing. But, more importantly, remember to keep giving thanks to God who created your life in the first place. Start when you wake up in the morning. Be thankful for the new day. The Bible says, *"This is the day the LORD has made, we will rejoice and be glad in it"* (Psalm 118:24 NLT).

Be thankful for being able to walk, talk, eat and drink. Be thankful for the place where you live; be thankful whether you are single or married; be thankful for your kids if you have children; be thankful for your family; be thankful for the country where you live. Write down a list of the things you have to be thankful for and look at it daily until you get the "thanks" habit. Stick the list on your fridge, your screensaver or the dashboard of your car.

Be Thankful for Your Work

Be thankful for your work. Work is a God-given means for earning money to live. If you really don't like your work and it's causing you stress, then get out of it. Life is too short for you to be doing something you hate. If you've been determined to make the best of it, you're of a likeable disposition and have a good attitude – and you still don't like it – then it may be time to go.

> **To get happy you need to start getting into the habit of giving thanks. Be thankful for everything you've got in life.**

Disliking your job is a big factor in blocking the potential of you getting the H Factor. You spend at least a third of your life doing it. I've always loved my work and I think I would have enjoyed whatever job I did. I love being a pastor. But equally I could have put my hand to and enjoyed being a businessman, a politician or almost any other profession.

I try to be thankful for the things I have and the things I go through in life. I give thanks for my wonderful wife, my great kids, my great friends, my nice car, my incredible physique . . . ! You get my point don't you! Seriously though, so many people end up hating their bodies. I'm usually a little bit overweight, but I enjoy the way God made me. I don't look like a bronzed Greek statue – more like a pale-skinned Buddha – but I like myself. I thank God for the body He has given me.

The Power of Thanksgiving

The United States is a big believer in the tradition of thanksgiving and, quite rightly, they celebrate the occasion big style.

Great! We all should! Earlier, in the J Factor chapter I told the story of when I was at the lowest point in my life. It sounds ridiculous, but I had to praise and give thanks, basically, to Almighty God, despite my whole world crashing around me. When I did, things instantly became better. There is something amazingly powerful about giving thanks to God, even when things are difficult. So next time you're in a sticky situation say, "Thank you God for just being who You are. Thank You for everything You have done for me. Thank You for making me. Thank You for how You're going to get me out of this problem. Thank You. Thank You!"

Try it and see what happens.

Life's Hurricanes Sometimes Blow

Most people see a hurricane blow through their life at one time or another. What I mean by a hurricane is an incident or set of incidents in life that rock our foundations to the core. Perhaps it is a phone call about a friend's death, a financial crisis or a marriage problem.

The thing about hurricanes we need to remember is that they always blow over. And that's the way to get through it. Focus on one day at a time. Whatever you do, don't think of the future and worry about it. The Bible tells us in Matthew 6 that it will take years off our lives. Be thankful for everything else in your life while the hurricane blows through.

Anne Frank, the German/Jewish teenager who was forced to go into hiding during the holocaust, said this: "I do not think of all the misery, but of the glory that remains. Go outside into the fields, nature and the sun, go out and seek happiness in yourself and in God. Think of the beauty that again and again discharges itself within and without you and be happy."

This little girl discovered a vital secret of happiness. Think and be thankful for the little things in your life. Don't focus on the negative aspects. And this is from a girl who lived in the middle of indescribable evil. It makes our hurricanes seem incredibly minor.

Don't Expect Thankfulness Back

One thing to remember is to be thankful to others but not necessarily expect thankfulness in return. That's a deadly game. However, you will reap what you sow. The only way to find happiness is to *not expect* gratitude, but to give for the joy of giving. It is natural for people to forget to be grateful, so, if we go around expecting gratitude, we are heading for heartache. Remember this little gem: expect little, give much. And whatever you do, don't get into the habit of discontentment. It will block your happiness.

Summary

1. Be thankful . . . for everything!
2. Practise being thankful
3. To be happy, be content
4. Don't expect thankfulness in return

The U Factor:
Uniqueness

"Today you are you, that is truer than true.
There is no one alive who is youer than you."
Dr Seuss (American writer and cartoonist)

"As we grow as unique persons,
we learn to respect the uniqueness of others."
Robert H. Schuller (American Reformed Church minister)

*"For you created my inmost being;
you knit me together in my mother's womb."*
The Bible (Psalm 139:13 NIV)

You are a one-off. You are brilliant. No one has ever been made like you in the history of the earth. You have the potential to achieve things in your life that no one else could possibly do. Why? Because you're unique.

Even after your mother and father mated, there was only a one chance in 300,000 billion that the person who is specifically you would be born. So if you had 300,000 billion brothers and sisters, you would still be unique! Furthermore, no one will ever be made that is like you again – probably! You were made in a particular way. You have had a unique background with unique parents and circumstances. You just couldn't be any more unique!

Celebrate your uniqueness. You have been made like that for a purpose. Life would be so much duller if we settled for all looking the same ... Life is exciting and you have a place to fit into it all.

I used to have a PA called Shane whose dress sense was the most appalling that you could find. He would come in with bright green luminous shirts, luminous orange ties, white trousers and trainers. I'd have to wear sunglasses while dictating my letters! He was unique and celebrated that fact. I'd tell him to be himself, and that's just what I'm saying to you now.

Celebrate your uniqueness

Celebrate your uniqueness. You have been made like that for a purpose. Life would be so much duller if we settled for all looking the same, sounding the same, wearing the same, doing the same things, having the same talents, and so on. Life is exciting and you have a place to fit into it all.

To get the H Factor you need to revel in your uniqueness. You need to find who you are, what your talents are, what motivates you, what your character is, what your dreams are, etc. Basically you have to be you – but first you need to discover who "you" really is. Who are you? Put down this book and think for a minute. Who are you really? Are you hiding under a mask or do you allow the real you to come out? Are you afraid of being rejected if you reveal who you really are? Be truthful. The liberating thing in life is being true to yourself. There is no gain at all in lying to yourself. If you aren't showing the real you, then free yourself by getting back to who the real you really is. Don't let others shape you. Many people – often those you consider friends – will be unnerved if you suddenly start to reveal the real you. But it is the best way to live.

You Were Made for a Reason

I'm just me. Yes, I'm often larger than life, I eat a bit too much, go over the top on occasion, have a tendency towards extremes, buy impulsively, make mistakes and fail to hit my goals. Yet, I still enjoy myself! I aim to be myself – even if others don't like that. I don't deliberately intend to upset anyone and obviously I try to display tact and sensitivity in certain settings – but most of the time I'm just me.

The whole world often seems to want to do the same thing. We dress the same and follow fashions. We follow the same football teams. We eat the same things. We expect church to be done in one particular way. That is dull, dull, dull! You were made for a reason. You were made for a purpose. God loves diversity. I passionately believe that you – and each and every one of us – were made by God in a particular way to be used to fulfil His purpose for our lives. Why not set fashions instead of following them!

To find out who the real you really is and what your talents are, answer these questions: what is your heart saying? Deep down what is your motivating passion in life? What are your experiences? What are your skills and abilities? What are your fears? You need to know these things to know yourself well.

Next you need to learn to love the unique you, warts and all. Many people dislike themselves and that's a tragedy. Signs of this include low self-esteem, a highly critical nature, an argumentative spirit, intolerance, excessive jealousy, an unforgiving attitude and great insecurities. How awful to go through life wishing you were someone else because you don't like yourself. I don't. I love being me and that doesn't mean I always like what I think, say and do. But you should love being you. God makes no mistakes. None. Not one. If I was you I'd enjoy being you too!

Enjoy Yourself

Once you know yourself, start to like yourself. Start to love yourself. I don't mean in a vain, arrogant, full of pride sort of way. I mean, value how Almighty God has made you. Know that God has made you unique and loves you that way. He loves you including the strengths and the weaknesses.

> **You should love being you.**
> **God makes no mistakes. None. Not one.**
> **If I was you I'd enjoy being you too!**

So many people are messed up by their unhealthy, difficult backgrounds. They were told by parents and peers that they were useless/ugly/thick/dozy/fat/thin and so on until they believed the lies. The lies sank into their subconscious so deep that they became a part of them. Are you like this? Then resolve to change before you finish this chapter. Life is too short to believe rubbish about yourself like that. It will destroy your life. Believing lies like this will stop you getting the H Factor.

But one point of caution. Don't blame your parents – or anyone else for that matter. Bitterness, even subconscious bitterness, will stop you getting the H Factor. You may need to forgive your parents – even if they are now dead – realize that you're not perfect and that no one is, and then move on in your life. You need to ask God to heal those hurts. If you have anger or bitterness deep down then deal with it now.

Tell yourself over and over that you are unique, that you're brilliant, that you have great skills and talents and you're going to use them the way God intended. Admit your weaknesses but focus on your strengths and be thankful for both. You're still lovable and likeable with weaknesses. Start to like your big nose because it's full of character. Admit you can't work with numbers and rejoice that you can spell well. Admit that you're not made to be the world's best orator and celebrate the fact that you can build a house.

Think Positively About Yourself

Again, this comes back to the mindset that we talked about in the chapter on Attitude. Start to reject the negative self-talk that goes on inside your head. Every time you hear yourself thinking that you're useless/ugly/thick/dozy/fat/thin etc., stop yourself and tell yourself that you're lovable, likeable, loved by God, just as you are. Remind yourself of your strengths and tell yourself that you don't need to be like everyone else to be okay. You are fine just as you are. You are unique!

If people reject you because you're being you, then that's their problem – not yours. Remember that. Tell yourself that. And one last point. Don't forget to accept the uniqueness of everyone else! Accept people the way they are and they'll love you for it. Everyone wants acceptance.

Start finding the real you. Find what you've uniquely been made to do and do it. Your ultimate happiness depends on it.

Summary

1. You are a unique person
2. Enjoy being you
3. Think positive thoughts about yourself
4. Celebrate your unique personality
5. Accept the unique personalities of others

CHAPTER 22

The V Factor:
Vision

"The most pathetic person in the world
is someone who has sight, but has no vision."
Helen Keller (American author)

"Vision is the art of seeing what is invisible to others."
Jonathan Swift (Irish author and satirist, 1667–1745)

"Where there is no vision, the people perish."
The Bible (Proverbs 29:18 KJV)

You need to have a vision of where you're going in life. Where are you going to be in fifty years time, in ten years time, in one year, in one month? This is your vision. Then you need goals which you will achieve in order to see your vision come to pass. Goals help you to get to where you want to be.

Psychologists have discovered that happiness is found whilst going after your goals. They have discovered, strangely, that people are happier when they know they are working towards their goals than when they achieve them! Yet, so many people I know fail to enjoy the journey and smell the coffee! That's why we continually need fresh goals, fresh vision – something new to drive for. Without goals and an overall vision your life will stagnate. The Bible says that without vision people perish (Proverbs 29:18). You will struggle to achieve happiness without having vision and some goals too.

A Reason for Living

I've seen it so often where people retire from their full-time occupation or wind down after achieving some wonderful project. Then they die. As I said in the chapter on Purpose, you need some reason for living. There's nothing worse than being washed up with no dream. It's a fast track to the grave. Nothing great was ever accomplished without having a vision. Every wonderful work of art, every stunning monument, each state-of-the-art wristwatch first had a vision that eventually became reality.

> **Nothing great was ever accomplished without having a vision. Every wonderful work of art, every stunning monument, each state-of-the-art wristwatch first had a vision that eventually became reality.**

On the day that Disneyworld was first opened, one man said that he wished Walt Disney had lived to see that great day. A fellow executive director replied to him, "he did." And that's the point. Walt had seen a vision of Disneyworld in his mind's eye before it was even built. That was vision. Your vision could be anything. It could be a vision to see a new skate park built in your neighbourhood. It could be a vision to get your kids into college, to lose two stones in weight, to buy a bigger house so you can show more hospitality, or even to ski down the French Alps! The vision is up to you.

Get Some Goals

Goals then need to be set. Goals need to be S-M-A-R-T. They need to be Specific, Measurable, Achievable, Relevant and Timed. So if you are overweight you could aim to lose one stone, which is specific and measurable. It should be achievable – this is something you need to assess carefully before you begin – and it is relevant to your life because, if you are a bit overweight, losing a stone will help you get fitter and healthier. Finally, it is important that your goal is timed. Set a realistic time limit to achieve what you want to achieve. It's no good saying you aim to lose a stone over the next ten years, for instance, because that would make it really difficult to monitor and the momentum of setting a goal and going for it would be lost.

When you've set your goals, write them down. I can't emphasise this strongly enough. Most people have a dream, a real passion for something, but goals are never set in order to get to that dream. Some people have a dream and they have goals, but they never write them down. This makes it very hard to monitor whether you are working towards and achieving your goals. Only a few people seem disciplined enough to crystallise their vision, set appropriate goals, and write down a plan setting out how they will achieve them. But there is real power in writing the goals down. According to research, the 3 percent of people who write down their goals achieve much more than the other 97 percent who don't write them down. It's not rocket science!

God Will Help You

Writing your goals down is one thing, but there is an even greater power in praying about your goals to God – and then letting Him help you to achieve them. Better still, why not let God guide your entire vision? God knows you and your future far better than you do! Let God help you get your vision. Write down goals to get there and then let God help turn them into a reality.

See Success – Not Failure

Think and pray over a mental picture of yourself as a success. Never think of yourself as failing. Never doubt the reality of the mental image. Visualise it and concentrate on it. A famous psychologist once said, "There is a deep tendency in human nature to become precisely like that which you habitually imagine yourself to be." So imagine yourself successful!

> **If you're failing to get the happiness habit
> in your life then check your vision.
> Do you have a big dream?
> If you don't, then find one.
> Everyone needs a dream.**

I've been amazed at the way my life has turned out. I thank God for the way He has guided me into new things, a wonderful wife, a great family, brilliant workplaces and superb churches. I want to be a man of great vision. I'm never happier than when having fresh vision for myself, my family or my church. Then a massive part of the fun is in helping to achieve that vision. That's where my goals come in.

If you're failing to get the happiness habit in your life then check your vision. Do you have a big dream? If you don't, then find one. Everyone needs a dream. Get the great book, *The Dream Giver*, by Bruce Wilkinson and go at it with all you've got. Until you've got a purpose and a vision you're aiming at nothing. The goals will be your roadmap. These things are vital for having the H Factor.

Summary

1. Work out what is your reason for living
2. Dream your dreams for your future, and decide on your vision
3. Set yourself goals which are S-M-A-R-T
4. Write down your goals
5. Work at achieving your goals
6. Get a mental picture of yourself as a success. Pray over it

The W Factor:
Wisdom

"Wisdom doesn't automatically come with old age.
Nothing does – except wrinkles. It's true, some wines
improve with age. But only if the grapes
were good in the first place."

Author unknown

"Never mistake knowledge for wisdom.
One helps you make a living;
the other helps you make a life."

Sandra Carey (author)

"If any of you lacks wisdom, he should ask God,
who gives generously to all without finding fault,
and it will be given to him."

The Bible (James 1:5 NIV)

There's one thing I've sought to get all my life – and that's wisdom. Even from my teenage years I can remember praying to God to give me wisdom. It doesn't sound that exciting, I know. It really doesn't seem like you would need wisdom to get overflowing happiness, but you do. Wisdom is one of the great keys to happiness.

A person without wisdom will hit stumbling blocks, guaranteed. A lack of wisdom can send you down the wrong path and it may mean a lot of pain. That is a barrier to happiness. Wisdom is the thing that keeps you from investing your life's savings in something stupid. Wisdom will keep you from going down the same lifestyle as the drug abuser. Wisdom is supreme. The Bible says, *"Therefore get wisdom"* (Proverbs 4:7 NIV). Lord Chesterfield once said to his son, "Be wiser than other people if you can, but do not tell them so."

More Is Less

The famous Greek philosopher Socrates said repeatedly to his followers in Athens, "One thing only do I know, and that is that I know nothing." You see, the one certain thing in life is that the longer we live the more questions we will have and the less we will know. If you think differently than this then that's arrogance. The opposite of arrogance is humility, and that is a wise path to follow.

> **Wisdom is to realize that you don't know it all, that you can't have all the answers and were never intended to.**

Don't Be Proud

The Bible says that God opposes the proud but gives grace to the humble (James 4:6). I've seen men and women fall big style because of having too much pride. God hates it. The saying "pride comes before a fall" is true (Proverbs 16:18). When you're proud you fail to seek good advice. That's unwise. Wisdom is to realize that you don't know it all, that you can't have all the answers and were never intended to. Wisdom is far more about "I know very little so help me" than "I know it all." The devil – who is the source of all evil in the world – was once an angel who was kicked out of heaven because he became proud. Pride is something that can affect us all. We want to take the glory. We want to be seen as amazing. We want people to look up at us and think how great we are. That's pride. That's not wisdom.

Humility Is Wisdom

Start right now to change your mindset and do away with pride. Realize that only Almighty God, Creator of heaven and earth is worthy of worship, praise and glory. You're not! I'm certainly not! I believe that others are better than I am. I believe that I'm a person who wants to have some answers, but very often fails to come up with the goods. I realize that as a person I fail continually. I don't always have success, but every day I give it my best shot. With God's help I'm getting better all the time. That's wisdom.

There's a famous prayer that is good to pray. It goes, "God grant me the serenity to accept the things I cannot change, the courage to change the things I can, and the wisdom to know the difference." This brings us to another point, that we really can't change everything in life. Knowing what we can change and knowing what we can't is one thing ... knowing the difference between the two is wisdom.

Very often people get frustrated, battered and bewildered by fighting constant battles to change things that can never be changed or don't really need changing. So we miss the bigger picture. We fail to focus on what is important. Wisdom is concentrating on the important things and putting a lower priority on the less important.

Get Your Priorities Right

I've mentioned this before but I'll mention it again because it is so important. If you want the H Factor, you're priorities in life should look like this: God first, your husband or wife second, the children third and then you're ministry or work fourth. No buts. No change. I've seen guys win huge success in their work, but lose their wife and family. What's the point in that? I had to learn the hard way on this one and regret some of my early married life when I worked seven days a week like a crazed horse. Ludicrous! I hope I've gained wisdom from this one and I hope you pick this one up – fast!

Be Teachable

Wisdom means that you're "teachable". It means that you realize you're learning every day until the day you die. This is so important and I look for it in people – the "teachable spirit". Wisdom is saying the right thing at the right time in the right manner with the right motive. Wisdom is knowing when to stop talking.

> **If you have a choice between education and wisdom, choose wisdom. If you have a choice between being a millionaire or having wisdom, choose wisdom. Wisdom will light your path. It will lead you to great things.**

When you're young you can often think you know it all. Teenagers often naturally lack wisdom, especially if they've had little wisdom input from parents, grandparents or teachers. But as you get older you can gain wisdom if you make a decision to learn from others and through life's circumstances. If you have a choice between education and wisdom, choose wisdom. If you have a choice between being a millionaire or having wisdom, choose wisdom. Wisdom will light your path. It will lead you to great things. It will lead you to the H Factor.

And remember, wisdom is not knowledge or intelligence. You can ask God for wisdom and that is different to the wisdom of man. Ask for it and seek it. You will find it (James 1:5).

Summary

1. Wisdom will keep you safe from trouble
2. The more you know, the more you realize that you don't know
3. Pride leads to failure
4. Develop a humble mindset
5. Accept the things that you can't change
6. Get your priorities in life right
7. Be teachable and always ready to learn from others
8. Prefer wisdom if your want to get the H Factor

CHAPTER

24

The X Factor:
The Cross

"Desire, ask, believe, receive."

Stella Terrill Mann

*"For God so loved the world that he gave his one and
only Son, that whoever believes in him shall not perish
but have eternal life."*

The Bible (John 3:16 NIV)

*"For 'whoever calls on the name of the LORD
shall be saved.'"*

The Bible (Romans 10:13 NKJV)

The X Factor isn't about talent. It's not that certain something
that some lucky people are born with. It's not a mix of character,
personality and talent that makes some people seem more
"special" than others. Neither do I mean a TV programme
designed to hunt down the nation's top singing talent. No. This
X Factor is far more important than that! It's life changing and
everyone can have it. It's also the icing on the cake of happiness.
If you take hold of the implications of the X Factor you've found
something very, very special. To put it simply, the X is a symbol

of love. The X is a symbol of destiny. And the X is a symbol of sacrifice.

I Got the X Factor

I was thirteen when I got the X Factor. It left me feeling on top of the world. I skipped home after finding it. It changed my life and things would never be the same again. It gave me a feeling of being totally and perfectly loved. It wasn't a girl or my mum that made me feel loved. At that age I wasn't married and I was too ugly to get a girlfriend! No, it was something different. Suddenly I knew that I had a destiny. I knew what I was meant to be doing. I also knew that a sacrifice had been made for me.

1. A Symbol of love

What is the X Factor?
X symbolises the cross of Christ – the cross that Jesus, God's Son, died on. Crucifixion on a wooden cross was the way the Romans executed people at that time. It was a long drawn out death unlike the electric chair! Why did He die? He had to die because of all the evil in the world. He died as a sacrifice for you and me. Why did God need a sacrifice? Well, it's all explained in the Bible, God's love-letter to us.

Why is there evil in the world?
The Bible tells us that we live in a world that was perfect when God made it. But, God's first two human creations, Adam and Eve, rebelled against Him and by doing so invited evil into the world. You can read about this in the book of the Bible called Genesis. This evil means that an evil force, which is the fallen angel called the Devil, was able to get a grasp on the world. A grasp that he still has.

What does this mean to us?

So where do you and I come in? Well, since Adam and Eve rebelled in the Garden of Eden, we have what is called "sin" within us. This sin is in us from birth and is the reason that we do wrong things. It includes things like getting angry, stealing, lusting after the next-door neighbour's new car or girlfriend, or failing to put God first in our lives.

Sin is summed up in the Bible's Ten Commandments (you can read about these in Exodus chapter 20 in the Bible) and is described wonderfully by J. John in his excellent book, *Ten*.[5] Now permit me to be blunt. What I'm about to say isn't always popular nowadays. It isn't cool. It isn't trendy. In fact some people see it as offensive. But it's the truth nevertheless so it needs to be said. Because you and I sin, we are what God calls "sinners". This means we are separated from God and cannot be in relationship with Him. To avoid this God needs a sacrifice for our sin. That sacrifice was Jesus.

A bit of history

In the ancient times, before Jesus was born, God could accept a sacrifice of a lamb or goat or whatever. But then about 2,000 years ago God came to earth in human form, called Jesus Christ. That's why we celebrate Christmas. Aged about thirty-three He was put to death, despite being perfect and never having committed any sin whatsoever. When He was led up to that cross (as we read in the books of Matthew, Mark, Luke and John in the Bible) He suffered a terrible death. That death, when He stretched His arms out wide and the nails were cruelly hammered through His hands, was for us. He died as a sacrifice for your sin, for my sin. Then three days later He rose from the dead and is alive today. That in a nutshell is the glorious truth.

---

[5] J. John, *Ten: Living the Ten Commandments in the 21st Century*, Kingsway, 2000.

The next step

All we need to do now to get the X Factor is first of all to believe this truth and then to say sorry to God for all the wrong we have done (see the prayer at the end of this chapter). After that we must follow Jesus Christ and accept all that He has done for us on the cross. This will save us from an eternity away from the presence of a loving God. Instead, we'll be off to spend eternity in heaven with God when we eventually leave this earth.

So what on earth has this to do with the H Factor, with getting happiness and living life to the full? Everything!

What happens now?

What does the H Factor mean? It means that you are fully happy and satisfied. It means you are an overcomer. It means that your happiness overflows to others and it means that you feel joy, satisfaction and pleasure. This is what the X Factor – Jesus' death on the cross – can do for you.

A number of things are accomplished for us when we fully accept Jesus' death on the cross. Jesus came to give us life to the full, above the ordinary, in abundance (see John 10:10 in the Bible). Jesus' death symbolises God's love for you – that He sent His only Son to die a terrible death on the cross so you could have eternal life (see John 3:16). The Bible tells us that He loves you so much that if you were the only person on earth He would still have died for you. You can't have the H Factor if your life knows no love.

2. You Have a Destiny

Furthermore, this death on the cross symbolises God's great plans for you; you have a destiny. By sending His Holy Spirit to be with you He now commissions you as His worker on earth to spread the message. The Holy Spirit gives you awesome God-given power to take on each and every day you face.

Many moons ago Napoleon wanted to conquer the world. He looked at a map and said, "If it wasn't for that red cross (which denoted Britain) I'd be able to conquer the world." That's what it's like with the Devil who gathers his evil forces around anything good and attempts to prevent us reaching new levels of happiness. But, Jesus' death on the cross defeated Satan once and for all. Though he has power now, it is limited and he is under God's overall control. Satan can do nothing without God's approval. So take the cross and cling to it, for Satan is defeated.

You are forgiven

The cross means that if you admit your sin and ask for forgiveness, then everything that you ever did which was wrong has been forgiven. The result is that you can now be free from guilt. That guilty feeling will just melt away as you realize that Jesus has been punished instead of you. You are forgiven.

The cross means that you now should be able to forgive others their sins. Unforgiveness, like worry and fear, is a great destroyer of happiness. Unforgiveness and resentment will block God from doing good things for you.

The cross also symbolises getting rid of all negativity. Its implications also mean an end to poverty and to illness. Jesus took everyone's sickness on the cross.

3. A Sacrifice

A new start

Basically for me, the X Factor is really what the H Factor is all about. It sums up complete and total happiness. Full stop. It's all there in the Bible. It is about a personal and very real relationship with the Creator through Jesus Christ. If there is no cross – no X Factor – then for me you can't have the full H Factor. It is an impossibility.

You will never be alone

One of the most powerful things to know in life is that God is actually with you and helping you. It could be said that no other knowledge is as powerful as this when put into practice. Just keep saying to yourself, "God is with me; God is helping me; God is guiding me." Visualise it and believe it. You will be amazed by the effect this will have on you.

> **If you take nothing else from this book, remember that God loves you so much that He gave His one and only Son to die for you, an excruciatingly painful and torturing death on the cross. That was for you.**

If you take nothing else from this book, remember that God loves you so much that He gave His one and only Son to die for you, an excruciatingly painful and torturing death on the cross. That was for you. If you give your life to Jesus today you will never be the same again. That's what I did aged just thirteen; what hundreds of million of people the world over have done. My life was changed for good and since then I've learnt to live life like an overcomer. I've learned to live life to the full. I've learned to live knowing that my life has divine purpose and that miracles are but a prayer away. Accept the X Factor and get the H Factor today.

Summary

1.   X symbolises love and the cross of Christ
2.   To really get the H Factor you also need the X Factor
3.   Jesus Christ died on the cross so that we can have a new life
4.   Get the X Factor so that you can find out what are the plans and the destiny God has already worked out for your life
5.   To get the X Factor, read this chapter and then say the prayer below to God

Prayer

"God forgive me for my sin, for turning away from You. Thank You for sending Jesus to die on the cross for me and for giving me eternal life. Come into my life and change me. Amen."

Follow Up

1.   Talk to God as much as possible
2.   Get a Bible in modern English and read it
3.   Get together with some other people who have also got the X Factor
4.   Contact us, and tell us about yourself, we want to hear from you.
     Email: johnp@edgechurch.com *or* info@hchurch.co.uk

The Y Factor: *Youthfulness*

25

"You can only be young once.
But you can always be immature."
Dave Barry

"Don't let anyone look down on you because you are young,
but set an example for the believers in speech,
in life, in love, in faith and in purity."
The Bible (1 Timothy 4:12 NIV)

"Don't let the excitement of youth cause you to forget your
Creator. Honor him in your youth before you grow old
and say, 'Life is not pleasant anymore.'"
The Bible (Ecclesiastes 12:1 NLT)

Keeping young is what we all seem to want. Women spend millions each year on beauty products to help keep them clear of wrinkles and reverse the ageing process. Many even invest tens of thousands of pounds on plastic surgery to help them stay looking young. Pop star Michael Jackson has allegedly spent millions trying to pursue his Peter Pan-style dream of staying young. Ridiculous. The truth is it doesn't cost a penny to keep young. It's possible to be an old person aged just twenty. It's also possible to be a young person aged eighty.

See Yourself As Young

One of the most vibrant, youthful, full-of-beans-type characters I've ever met is a great friend of mine called Nancy. At eighty-four years she is still very youthful. She is just a wonderful lady. At our church she swept the floors, made the tea, served in the café, cleaned the rooms, volunteered for everything, out-danced people a quarter her age, and holidayed around the world with the best of them. Why could she do this? Because of her mindset. She had an inner attitude that thought and acted young. You can do the same.

Another lady I know called Anne resolved to keep young. She tried to keep that spirit of playfulness into her sixties. She tried not to celebrate birthdays because others would speak her into feeling old. Instead she would think how young she felt, how youthful she was, how much energy she had. Even though she was an old age pensioner she looked at least twenty years younger than her identity card said. A wonderful woman! See yourself as young and you'll change the way you feel. Youthfulness keeps you smiling, fun-loving and non-prejudiced.

Children Love Fun

I feel like a teenager on the inside. I may not be the fittest I've ever been, but I'm enthusiastic about life, just like a child. Children are wonderful. God Himself said in the Bible that we need to become like little children to get into heaven. Children don't see black people and white people – they see only people. That's the way it should be. Children love fun. They play – lots!

Children love skipping, chuckling and taking risks. When was the last time you did these things? Young people have the spirit of adventure. They anticipate the hope of a better tomorrow. Both are necessary requirements for getting the H Factor. Have you got these qualities?

> **Children love skipping, chuckling and taking risks.**
> **When was the last time you did these things?**
> **Young people have the spirit of adventure.**
> **They anticipate the hope of a better tomorrow.**

At times in my life people have asked when I am going to "grow up". My answer is always "Never!" I love being playful, youthful and having a childlike spirit. Remember, you can still be youthful and wise. It's just great to act silly at times, to let your hair down and have some childlike fun.

The Benefits of Staying Young

Consider the benefits. Being young at heart means you'll feel younger. Experts say that you can think yourself to a healthy body. It will show on your face. You'll have more energy, more friends and more enjoyment in life. People want to be around those who are playful and fun to be with. Do you allow your birth certificate to determine your level of fun? Then stop it now. Rip it up if needs be and be eternally young! One of the pioneers of positive thinking, Norman Vincent Peale, stayed vibrant into his mid-nineties. He knew the truth that your thoughts make you what you are. So he stayed in love with his wife, kept his thoughts on good things and resolved to play and adventure like a child would.

Throw Off Your Old Mindset

I meet so many people who grow old before their time. We've been given a very short time on earth, an average of seventy something years, so don't waste it wanting to be older than you are – or younger than you are either! Vow to die feeling as young as you did in your teens.

> **People want to be around those who are playful and fun to be with. Do you allow your birth certificate to determine your level of fun?**

Of course, if you insist on smoking, excessive drinking, stress and an unhealthy diet, then that will play its part on cutting short your allotted time. But, your mindset will have a massive role. Don't let your mindset rob you of your youth. Start to imagine yourself as young. Throw off your old mindset and attitudes of being old. You're not! Your "peak" years are when you're at your best. Determine to be the sort of person who ends their years with a childlike spirit. There's no better way to be.

Summary

1. Act young
2. Be around young at heart type people
3. Remember the benefits of staying young
4. Stay fun loving!

The Z Factor:
Zest

"If you have zest and enthusiasm you attract zest and
enthusiasm. Life does give back in kind."
Norman Vincent Peale

"True happiness comes from the joy of deeds well done,
the zest of creating things new."
Antoine de Saint-Exupery

*"Love the Lord your God with all your heart and
with all your soul and with all your mind."*
Jesus (Matthew 22:37 NIV)

Z may be last in this book but Zest has to be one of the first
components needed for getting the H Factor. What is it that
generates your drive in life? Zest. What is it that gives you
energy? Zest.

Zest is defined in the dictionary as the same as excitement
and is characterised by enthusiasm, eagerness and energy – all
characteristics of someone with the H Factor. Think of someone you know who is a bit of a "down and out". They walk
slowly. They don't quite know where to go or what to do.
There is a quenched spirit in them. They almost let life pass

them by. Unemployed people, the homeless, aimless people, drug addicts and alcoholics can be like this, although not always or automatically so. Tragically, somewhere in life they lost that childhood zest for life – the zest that we are all born with.

As babies we have a zest to learn to walk. As children we have a zest to learn and grow and enjoy life. Then somewhere along the line, many of us lose that zest and allow dullness and depression to cloud our lives. Perhaps our parents held up too high expectations we could never live up to and we felt like failures. Perhaps we never felt loved. Perhaps we were abandoned by a parent, carer, girlfriend or employer. Often when things wound people in life they turn to alcohol, drugs or other pursuits designed to numb the pain. People who do that end up hating life. They lose their zest for it because they hurt too much on the inside.

If that in any way describes you or what you've been through, you need to know today that you can have a zest for life again. God intends for you to live life like a child does – eagerly expectant of every day, hardly able to sleep because of the excitement in store from simply living.

Change Your Life to Zest

We'll learn how to change your life around and live with zest in this chapter. Think of those you know who are going places. They have a purpose and goals and know what they're doing. These type of people have the H Factor. They have enthusiasm, eagerness and energy. They have zest. They walk with a bounce, show enjoyment in the way they live, are eager for new challenges and are passionate people. People like Virgin owner Richard Branson and film star Arnold Schwarzenegger have the Z factor, and so did the late, great "Crocodile Hunter" Steve Irwin.

We often say that certain people have a "zest for life" and they approach tasks with a boundless energy. We mean that they really are enthusiastic for the next challenge. Enthusiasm lifts living out of the depths and makes it mean something. Play it cool and you will freeze! Play it hot and even if you get it wrong and get burned, at least you will have shed a bit of warmth over a discouraged and bewildered world! That's how we need to live in order to have the H Factor. I think people who know me will know that I carry this zest for life wherever I go. I just can't get enough of it.

Billy Graham Has Zest

Others that have it include most people who achieve anything of note in this world. Think of anti-poverty campaigner and Band Aid pop concert organiser Bob Geldof. This guy has zest. Think of the leader of Australia's fastest growing church, Brian Houston or the famous evangelist Billy Graham. These guys have zest. Think of past go-getting world leaders such as George Bush, Tony Blair and Margaret Thatcher – they all had an overwhelming zest for life. You can have it too. Whatever your current situation, get enthused because you can become a man or woman of zest.

> **Enthusiasm lifts living out of the depths and makes it mean something. Play it cool and you will freeze!**

The source of the word zest is the Greek word *enthousiasmos* from which we get the English word "enthusiasm" and ultimately comes from the adjective *entheos*, which means literally "God within". Almighty God wants you enjoying life and living with zest. The Bible tells us that God sent His Son Jesus to earth so that we can have life to the full, a wonderful zest for living. See John 10:10 in the Bible for proof of this.

God Wants You to Have Zest

The Creator built energy into you and me when we were born. He implanted within us a life force and true faith can keep this life force alive. If you don't have this then you're not living how God wants you to live. You see, God loves you with an incredible love. He wants you to love Him too and to make Him the object of your main affection. The Bible tells us that the main things God values is that we love Him first and then other people around us. The Bible also wants you to be living a full life, enjoying it in every way. Incidentally, as we learnt in the F Factor, God also loves it when you laugh and show how much you enjoy life.

To get this zest for life, I believe in these three things: loving, living (life to the full) and laughing. If we live this way we really will have zest and the places where we live, work, and go to church will be transformed. Families will be happy places, marriages will thrive, workplaces will be buzzing, people will enjoy their work and churches will be crammed full all across the nations.

Watch Your Family Flourish with Zest

If you are in a family, workplace or church, try injecting a bit of this zest for living into the culture of the place. Watch the family flourish. Watch your workplace become a happier place to be. See your church overflow with people and life. Go at life with abandon, give it all you've got, and life will give all it has back to you.

Wherever I've been, the atmosphere has turned into one of zest and I've always had great churches and found myself surrounded by great people. I've always had great work situations. And, though the family has been through its ups and downs, I've always enjoyed my family. It's never without a bit of fun and zest. If your family is struggling, your workplace dull and your church dying then do your best to regain your zest and spread it around. It's highly contagious! The world needs more of it. Remember the "fishing philosophy"? Have fun, be there, make their day and choose your attitude!

So what if you're so full of pain and hurt that you can't possibly think of zest? That's where Almighty God comes in.

God Loves You

Like I said, God created you and loves you with a perfect love. He really wants you to be healed emotionally of all the hurts and hates that can plague our lives. We can't possibly have zest and look forward to life if we carry this baggage around with us. You need to hand all your life and all your problems and all your hurts over to this loving God of the Bible. Believe that He can turn your life around and begin to develop a buzz within you that is contagious. I know He can.

Pray to God. Prayer is simple. It is communicating with God involving speaking and listening. Try it now. Say something like,

> "Almighty God, I want to know You. I want You to come into my life and heal my hurts. I am sorry for living for myself rather than You all these years. Please forgive me. Help me to have a zest for life. Help me to have the H Factor. Thank You for sending your Son, Jesus Christ, to die for me, and the Holy Spirit to live within me. I ask these things in Jesus' name."

If you prayed that prayer your life will already be different. God will begin a process in you that will help to grow you every day of your life. Partner with God to help Him develop that zest within you. Think big, pray big, live big, believe big, love big, serve big, give big. Be big in soul. Health and prosperity depend upon the soul, and the soul depends upon God.

Pray every day that your relationship with God will grow. Pray that you'll live a life worthy of a follower of Jesus and you'll soon be living a life of overflowing zest ... a life characterised by the H Factor.

Summary

1. We are all born with a natural zest for life
2. Great achievers have zest
3. We can regain that lost zest by loving, living and laughing
4. Almighty God – through His Son Jesus Christ – can help you

Contact Details

www.getthehfactor.com
info@hchurch.co.uk
johnp@edgechurch.com

We hope you enjoyed reading this New Wine book.
For details of other New Wine books
and a range of 2,000 titles from other
Word and Spirit publishers visit our website:
www.newwineministries.co.uk